KRISTEN PARKER

The Hollow Song of Eternity

Copyright © 2025 by Kristen Parker

All rights reserved. No part of this publication may be reproduced, stored or transmitted in any form or by any means, electronic, mechanical, photocopying, recording, scanning, or otherwise without written permission from the publisher. It is illegal to copy this book, post it to a website, or distribute it by any other means without permission.

This novel is entirely a work of fiction. The names, characters and incidents portrayed in it are the work of the author's imagination. Any resemblance to actual persons, living or dead, events or localities is entirely coincidental.

Kristen Parker asserts the moral right to be identified as the author of this work.

Kristen Parker has no responsibility for the persistence or accuracy of URLs for external or third-party Internet Websites referred to in this publication and does not guarantee that any content on such Websites is, or will remain, accurate or appropriate.

Designations used by companies to distinguish their products are often claimed as trademarks. All brand names and product names used in this book and on its cover are trade names, service marks, trademarks and registered trademarks of their respective owners. The publishers and the book are not associated with any product or vendor mentioned in this book. None of the companies referenced within the book have endorsed the book.

First edition

*This book was professionally typeset on Reedsy.
Find out more at reedsy.com*

One

The Song That Calls

Selisyn Oriah had always believed that the world was bound by time—that everything, even love, would fade or be torn apart by the ceaseless passage of moments. Yet as she walked through the forest, there was no evidence of time's hold. The trees loomed around her, their gnarled branches reaching out like ancient hands, their leaves unfurling in a way that defied the seasons. The air was thick with the scent of moss and damp earth, a timeless freshness that clung to her skin and wrapped itself around her senses.

The sun, though overhead, seemed suspended, its light neither growing brighter nor dimming as the minutes passed. She had long lost track of time, her thoughts drifting in and out like the wind. But something had changed. A pull, subtle at first, had wormed its way into her chest, tugging her toward something unknown, something primal. It was as though the forest itself had whispered a secret, and Selisyn, despite the unease curling in her stomach, couldn't resist listening.

It started softly—barely audible above the rustling of the trees—a faint, almost imperceptible melody. A single note that floated in the air like the fleeting echo of a dream. It was beautiful, a harmony that seemed to vibrate with something deeper than sound, something almost alive. It echoed in her mind, weaving through her thoughts like a siren's call. Every step she took seemed to bring her closer, as though the song itself was pulling her forward.

Her breath quickened. The forest had shifted around her in a way that she couldn't place. The landscape remained unchanged, but the air felt thicker now, as though it carried a weight she had not noticed before. The trees were darker, their trunks coated in an eerie sheen, and the ground beneath her feet had become softer, almost springy as if it could swallow her whole. Yet, the melody beckoned, unwavering.

It was both beautiful and unsettling, its notes carrying a faint sense of melancholy, a sadness that scraped at the edges of her consciousness. With each step, her heart beat faster, quicker, the rhythm of her pulse aligning with the haunting tune. It felt wrong, and yet, it felt right. The melody, with its gentle cadences and aching sweetness, gripped her, drawing her deeper into the forest as if it knew her every fear, every longing.

Then, as though the forest had finally decided to reveal its mystery, the source of the song became apparent.

Up ahead, by a shimmering, endless pool of water, stood a figure. His back was to her, and he was staring out across the water, his hands at his sides, his posture rigid but serene. The song was louder here, vibrating the very air around her, and it emanated from him as though his very soul was entwined with the melody.

She froze.

It was as though the world had paused. For a moment, there was no sound—the hum of the forest, the song, the beat of her own heart—all of it vanished in an instant. Her breath caught in her throat.

He turned.

It was then that the world seemed to shift. His gaze, when it met hers, was like the sudden rush of a summer storm. Dark eyes locked onto hers with such intensity that she stumbled backward, her heart leaping into her throat. She had known him.

She hadn't known him at all.

The stranger before her was as much a part of this strange forest as the trees, as the song that had led her here. His features were sharp, sculpted with a beauty that seemed unearthly, as though he had been carved by gods who had long since forgotten their creations. His hair, black as midnight, hung loose around his shoulders, a stark contrast to the pale skin that seemed almost ethereal, glowing faintly in the dim light.

She felt the magnetic pull between them, so strong that it felt like it had always been there, lurking beneath the surface of her thoughts. She was certain of it—this man, this stranger, had always been a part of her life, had always been a part of her.

He blinked, as though shaken out of a trance, and for the briefest moment, the tension in the air seemed to snap. His voice, when it came, was soft, a deep and velvety baritone, tinged with a foreign accent that felt both comforting and strange.

"You hear it too, don't you?" he asked, his voice barely more than a whisper, the words hanging between them like a fragile thread.

Selisyn nodded, her throat too dry to speak. She could feel the song vibrating through her body now, pulling at her chest, like it was trying to break free from within her. The more she listened, the less she understood. The melody was both her salvation and her undoing.

"I thought I was the only one," he continued, his eyes never leaving hers. There was something unsettling in the way he spoke, something like a confession, though she couldn't yet place it. "It's been... hours? Days? I can't remember." He paused, almost as if trying to recall something he had lost. "But you—" He took a step closer, his eyes flickering with something unreadable. "You shouldn't be here."

The last words hung in the air, cold and haunting, like a warning she couldn't fully grasp. But she wasn't afraid. No, she felt something else—curiosity, a wild need to understand, to know what this pull meant.

"You're not from here," she finally managed, her voice trembling as she found her courage. The words felt heavy, like they were not her own, but they spilled from her mouth regardless.

The stranger tilted his head, a slight smile tugging at the corners of his lips, though it was faint, barely there. "Neither are you," he said, his gaze shifting to the pool of water behind him. The water shimmered like liquid glass, reflecting the pale light of a distant, unseen moon.

Selisyn's breath hitched. The water—it was strange, almost unnatural. It didn't ripple as water should. It was as if the pool was frozen in time, the surface smooth and still, as though it held secrets far older than the world itself.

The Song That Calls

For a moment, neither of them spoke. The only sound was the haunting song, growing louder, as though it was aware of their presence, aware of their shared connection.

Then, with a slow and deliberate movement, the stranger extended his hand toward her. "I'm Thalior Myrren," he said softly, his fingers almost brushing hers. "And you, Selisyn Oriah, are far from home."

Selisyn froze. The mention of her name felt like a shock, an electric pulse that zipped through her veins. Her eyes widened, confusion clouding her mind. How could he possibly know her name? She had never seen this man before in her life. She stepped back, her heart hammering in her chest.

"How do you know my name?" she asked, her voice strained with disbelief.

Thalior's face softened, his brow furrowing slightly. "I don't know," he said quietly, as though the answer itself confused him. "But I know it. I've known it for as long as I've known the song."

The words settled in her mind like fragments of a puzzle, each piece shifting into place but not quite fitting. She had never heard of him. Never seen his face. And yet, in the deepest recesses of her being, she could feel him as if he had always been a part of her life.

The song—still singing, still calling, growing more intense—began to pulse around them, filling the air with a presence that was both beautiful and terrifying.

Selisyn turned toward the pool again, her eyes scanning the shimmering surface. For the first time, she noticed something strange—a figure beneath the water, flickering just beneath the surface, as though it was watching her. She gasped, stepping back.

Thalior's eyes followed her gaze, a shadow crossing his face. "Do not look too long," he murmured, his voice suddenly strained. "That is not a reflection. It is a warning."

Selisyn's pulse quickened. She felt her heart race, the need to understand consuming her. "What is it?" she whispered.

Thalior didn't answer right away. His gaze was distant, as though he were seeing something she couldn't. "It's what keeps us here," he said softly. "The song isn't just a song. It's a prison."

A prison.

Selisyn swallowed hard, her mind reeling. Was this place—this timeless, ageless forest—a prison? And if so, why had it called to them? Why had it pulled her here, to this stranger with eyes that seemed to hold the weight of centuries?

"I don't understand," she whispered, the words barely audible.

Thalior's voice, when it came, was barely a breath. "Neither do I."

The forest hummed, alive with the pulse of the song, and Selisyn felt an overwhelming sense of both dread and wonder. She realized, in that moment, that her life had just changed forever. There was no going back.

And the song would never let them go.

Certainly! Here's a continuation of the chapter to make it more immersive and further develop the tension and mystery:

Selisyn stood frozen, the weight of Thalior's words sinking into her mind like the slow, rhythmic pulse of the song. *A prison.* She tried to understand it, to make sense of the words, but they didn't fit with what her senses were telling her. This place, the song, the water—none of it made sense. She had no memory of how she had arrived here, but she felt in her bones that she was tied to this world in some way she couldn't explain.

Her heart thundered in her chest, and yet, despite the fear rising within her, she felt something else—something that made her feel grounded, as if she had been waiting for this moment for lifetimes. She glanced at Thalior again. His eyes were no longer focused on her. Instead, they were fixed on the water, a shadow passing over his face.

"Thalior…" she began, but her voice faltered. She wasn't sure what to say. There were too many questions, too many layers of confusion. The only certainty was that she could not ignore the feeling inside her, that deep ache, as if something in her had been waiting for him.

But she wasn't ready to admit that yet.

"Why are we here?" she finally managed to ask, her voice quivering with the weight of the unknown.

Thalior didn't answer immediately. His lips pressed together in a thin line, and his eyes flickered to the pool again. The figure beneath the water seemed to writhe, its form distorting, though it was barely visible. The more she stared, the more it seemed to shift, a shadow tangled in the glassy surface. Her pulse quickened, but she couldn't look away. There was something almost hypnotic about it. The way it seemed to call to her—pulling at something deep inside her that she didn't understand.

His words were almost too quiet to hear over the hum of the song, but when he spoke, his voice was rough, as though the very act of speaking was a struggle. "This place… it's not a place at all. It's a… crossing. Between worlds, between lives. A place suspended in time." He hesitated, his eyes glinting with the same haunting, mysterious depth that seemed to swallow him whole. "And the song... it's the only thing that can lead us out. But we must listen. Truly listen. Only then will we understand how to escape."

"Escape?" The word felt wrong on her tongue, as though she had been told something she wasn't meant to know. "Escape from what?"

The eerie, mournful tune seemed to swell in intensity, vibrating the ground beneath her feet. For a moment, she was sure the earth itself was about to crack open.

Thalior stepped closer to the water's edge, his gaze fixed downward. "This world, the one we're in... it doesn't exist. Not in the way we know it. It's as if it's frozen, a moment in time that's never moved forward. No beginning. No end. No escape unless..." His voice trailed off, and his eyes flashed toward her, filled with something that almost looked like fear.

"Unless what?" Selisyn demanded, her voice sharp now, more insistent. She needed answers. The tension between them, thick and electric, seemed to crackle in the air like a storm waiting to break. She could feel the pressure building—something inside her urging her to push further.

"Unless we stop fighting it," Thalior said, almost bitterly. "Unless we accept that time, as we know it, doesn't apply here. This is the hollow space. The space between the moments, between lives. And the song is the thread, the only thing keeping us from becoming like the others."

"Others?" Her throat tightened, the word unfamiliar yet terrifying. She had no idea what he was talking about, but she knew she didn't want to find out.

"Yes," Thalior murmured. He closed his eyes for a brief moment, as if summoning the strength to speak. "We are not the first to hear the song, Selisyn. We are not the first to be drawn here." His words were thick, almost drowned out by the music that continued to rise around them, pulsing and thrumming through the very air. "Others have come before us. They've followed the call, too. Some of them... they never left."

She could feel her stomach twist at the thought. The implication was clear: *they had stayed. They had been lost to the song, lost to the place.*

"But we're different." He turned to face her fully, his eyes boring into hers with an intensity that made her breath hitch. "You're different. I don't know how or why, but I've... I've been here longer than I can remember. I've heard the song over and over again, waiting for someone like you."

Her heart skipped a beat. "Someone like me?"

Thalior nodded, his expression unreadable. "Yes. Someone who will hear it in the way I hear it. Someone who can... unravel its secrets."

A chill swept through her, one colder than anything she had ever felt, and yet there was something else there—an invitation, a promise. A chance to understand.

The song swelled again, louder now, as if it were wrapping itself around her very soul, pulling her in deeper.

Selisyn reached out, her fingers trembling as she touched the edge of the pool. The water was smooth and still, but the surface rippled as though it could feel her touch. She jerked her hand back, startled by the sudden movement. Her reflection in the water had changed—twisted, distorted. The face staring back at her was not her own but something older, something unfamiliar.

Thalior's voice broke the silence. "It's showing you. Showing us. The past... the future... the lives we've lived before. The song… it's more than just a melody. It's a thread, a bridge, a key to understanding what we are, and what we've been."

He stepped closer, his eyes dark and full of secrets. "And what we will be."

Selisyn's breath caught. "What do you mean? What do you see?"

Thalior looked at her, a strange sadness passing over his face. "I see us. Together. Here, in this place. The song is meant to keep us trapped, to make us forget. But it can also set us free. We must break it."

"How do we do that?" Her voice was desperate now, the urgency in her chest growing with each passing second. The song was growing louder, more demanding, its notes wrapping around her like tendrils, squeezing her heart.

Thalior's eyes darkened. "By remembering. By *believing*. This place is not just a prison for time. It's a prison for the soul. We can break it, but we must first understand why we were chosen to hear it, why it calls to us."

A sudden gust of wind stirred the stillness of the air, and the song shifted, its tone deepening, warping into something darker. It no longer sounded like a call for salvation; it sounded like a warning.

"Selisyn…" Thalior's voice was strained now, his gaze flickering with something darker. "There's something else. Something we haven't fully realized yet. The song… it isn't just for us. It's for them too. The ones who never left. The ones who are waiting for us to join them."

Her stomach turned. "Them?"

"The lost souls," he whispered. "The ones who failed to break free. They are here, in the water. Waiting for us to fail, to join them in the endless cycle of time."

The Song That Calls

Selisyn's eyes widened as she stared at the pool again, her heart hammering in her chest. She could see them now—shadows moving beneath the water, faces she couldn't quite make out, but whose gazes pierced into her soul. Their eyes were empty, hollow, like echoes of forgotten memories. She gasped, stumbling back, her legs weak beneath her.

"They're coming," Thalior said, his voice low, filled with urgency. "They're drawn to us. To the song. To what we represent. We need to leave. Now."

But it was too late.

The water began to churn, its surface twisting and writhing like something alive. The shadows beneath it began to rise, first slowly, then faster. Selisyn's heart stopped as she saw them—the figures, their faces twisted in agony, their bodies half-formed, flickering like reflections in a cracked mirror. The song had changed, and so had the forest around them. Time, once again, was slipping away.

Thalior grabbed her arm, pulling her toward the edge of the forest. "We can't let them pull us under, Selisyn. If they do, we will never escape. Never."

With every step, the figures drew closer. The water surged, as though it had become sentient, alive with the souls of the lost.

Selisyn's breath was ragged, her mind struggling to grasp the horror unfolding before her. The song, the water, the souls—they were all connected. They were all part of the same nightmare, and the only way to survive was to break the cycle.

She looked at Thalior, her heart heavy with the weight of the unknown. "How?"

Thalior didn't answer. He just pulled her into the depths of the forest, away from the pool, away from the song.

The Hollow Song of Eternity

But she could still hear it. The song. Still calling. Still waiting.

And the deeper they went, the stronger the pull.

Two

The Realm of Forever

The air around Selisyn was thick with stillness. The moment she stepped forward, a strange sense of displacement filled her, as though the ground beneath her feet was not quite real. There was no warmth from the sun, no breeze that ruffled the leaves above. The forest, with its towering trees and undisturbed silence, seemed to stretch endlessly in every direction, an expanse of shadow and light that didn't obey the rules of nature. It was as though she had stepped into a place outside of time, a world suspended between moments.

Beside her, Thalior moved with the same caution, his every step measured, as if testing the ground beneath him. She caught the briefest flicker of tension in his features, an unspoken fear reflected in his eyes. He was as unsettled as she was. Neither of them had spoken since they fled from the pool, both lost in their thoughts, each struggling to make sense of the impossible world around them.

Selisyn reached out and touched the nearest tree. Its bark was smooth beneath her fingertips, but it was cold—unnaturally so, as if the life within the wood had been drained. When she drew her hand back, she noticed something strange: there was no mark left on the tree. No impression of her touch, no trace of her presence. It was as though the world itself was erasing her.

"Do you feel it?" she asked quietly, her voice hoarse from the surreal tension that hung in the air.

Thalior didn't answer immediately. His gaze was distant, his brow furrowed as though he, too, was struggling to comprehend the sensation. Then he spoke, his voice low, barely audible.

"I've felt it before," he said, his tone hollow. "This place. It's endless. It's as if time doesn't exist here."

Selisyn shivered, though she couldn't tell if it was from the cold air or the weight of his words. She swallowed hard, her throat dry. The memory of the pool—the water, the song, the shadows—still clung to her like a second skin. The echo of the melody, faint but undeniable, buzzed in her ears. It was louder now, and though it had no origin, it seemed to grow in intensity with every step they took.

"Where are we?" she asked, her voice barely above a whisper. The question felt wrong to even ask. The world they were in had no answer. There were no landmarks, no signposts, no indication of direction. She felt disoriented, lost in a place that defied all logic.

Thalior's gaze shifted to the horizon, where the trees gave way to an endless expanse of mist. "I don't know," he replied, his voice strained. "But I've been here before. I've wandered this forest for… for as long as I can remember. I know every tree, every stone, and yet it's different this time. I can feel it."

Selisyn's heart thudded in her chest, the rhythm of it a stark contrast to the eerie silence of the forest. "You've been here before?" she asked. "But you don't remember how you got here?"

Thalior nodded, his expression grim. "Exactly. It's like… like a loop. A cycle I can't escape. I've tried everything. I've followed the song, followed the pull, but every path leads back here. Every time, I come back to this place."

She stared at him, her breath catching in her throat. She didn't understand it, but she could feel the truth of his words deep within her. This world—they were trapped in it. There was no way out.

"I—" Selisyn began, but she was interrupted by the sound of the song rising again, its notes swelling, more insistent now, like a warning. It wrapped around her, pulling her deeper into its pull. "The song…" She paused, her thoughts scattered. "It's getting louder. Why?"

Thalior looked at her, his eyes wide with something like recognition. "It's because you're with me," he said softly. "It's because we're together."

Selisyn's stomach lurched. "What does that mean?"

He shook his head, frustration creeping into his voice. "I don't know. But every time I've come here, every time I've heard the song, I've been alone. Now, with you… it's different."

The ground beneath them seemed to shudder slightly, and Selisyn glanced down, startled. The earth was shifting, as if the very fabric of the world around them was alive. Her breath quickened as she stepped back, her heart racing.

"Thalior," she said, her voice tight. "What if we're not

supposed to be here?"

The question hung in the air between them like an unspoken truth, an ominous weight. But before he could answer, a rustling sound broke through the silence, snapping her out of her thoughts. Something was moving in the distance, just beyond the trees. The air seemed to ripple with an unseen energy.

"Stay close," Thalior said, his voice low but urgent.

Without thinking, Selisyn obeyed, her heart pounding in her chest as she stepped closer to him. The tension between them had shifted, their proximity creating an invisible barrier, a bond that was both unfamiliar and undeniable. It wasn't just the pull of the song now. There was something more, something deep and ancient between them that was beginning to make itself known.

The rustling grew louder, and then, from the shadows between the trees, a figure appeared.

It was tall, cloaked in a dark robe that seemed to shimmer with a faint, otherworldly glow. His face was hidden in shadow, but there was no mistaking the presence that radiated from him. The moment he stepped forward, Selisyn could feel the air around her grow thick with power.

"Who are you?" Thalior demanded, his voice sharp.

The figure raised his hand in a gesture of calm, his movements slow and deliberate. "I am Vorrin Elestra," he said, his voice rich and deep, carrying the weight of centuries. "And I am the one who has watched over this realm for as long as time has forgotten."

Selisyn's pulse quickened as she exchanged a glance with Thalior. Neither of them had ever seen this being before, but there was an undeniable sense of recognition, as if he was somehow tied to their presence here. The way he spoke—it was as though he knew them, knew everything about them.

"You are trapped," Vorrin continued, his gaze fixed on them both. "Just as I once was. Just as all who wander into the realm of forever are. The song, it binds you here. And it is through the song that you will find your way out."

Selisyn's mind reeled. "The song?" she echoed. "But what is it? Why does it call to us?"

Vorrin's eyes glinted in the dim light, something unreadable flickering in them. "The song is the key," he said, his voice low, like the rustling of leaves in a storm. "It is the melody that threads through time itself, binding souls, weaving destinies. It is a song of creation and destruction. A song that does not belong to this world, nor to the next."

"Then why does it pull us in?" Thalior asked, his voice rising with desperation. "Why does it make us feel—" He paused, as if searching for the right words. "Why does it make us feel like we're meant to be here? Together?"

Vorrin tilted his head, as though considering Thalior's question. "Because you are meant to be here," he said softly. "Not by chance. Not by fate. But by design."

Selisyn felt her breath catch in her throat. "What do you mean?"

Vorrin's gaze shifted to her, his eyes sharp and knowing. "You, Selisyn, and you, Thalior, are more than you appear. You are bound by the song, by the very essence of time itself. The love you feel—it is no accident. It is what will break the cycle."

Thalior stepped forward, his jaw clenched in frustration. "But we don't even know what that means! How can we break the cycle when we don't even understand it?"

"You will," Vorrin said, his voice a whisper now. "In time. But first, you must learn what it means to love in a world where time does not exist. Only then can you break the song's hold."

Selisyn's mind raced, trying to grasp what Vorrin was saying. A world without time. A love that could break a cycle. Her thoughts twisted, but the image of Thalior standing beside her, his presence a constant pull, kept her grounded.

"What do we have to do?" she asked, her voice a little stronger now.

Vorrin's lips curled into a knowing smile. "First, you must understand that the song has two faces. One of creation, one of destruction. And the only way to free yourselves… is to embrace both."

Thalior shook his head, confusion and fear creeping into his expression. "What do you mean, embrace both?"

Vorrin's eyes darkened, and for the first time, Selisyn saw something resembling pity in them. "You will see. In time. But know this: The cycle will break only when the love between you is tested. Only then will the song cease its eternal call."

Without another word, Vorrin turned and disappeared into the shadows of the forest, his presence fading as quickly as it had come.

Selisyn stood in stunned silence, her mind spinning with his words. Thalior remained motionless beside her, the weight of the moment pressing down on them both.

"What does it mean?" Selisyn whispered, her voice trembling. "How can we break the song when we don't even understand it?"

Thalior's gaze locked with hers, his eyes filled with a mix of fear, determination, and something else she couldn't quite name.

"I don't know," he said, his voice thick with emotion. "But

we'll find a way."

And as the last notes of the Eternal Song echoed in the distance, they turned to face the endless forest ahead.

Time, it seemed, was no longer their enemy. It was the very thing they needed to unravel if they were to escape.

They stood there for a moment, the words from Vorrin still hanging in the air, thick with meaning and unspoken danger. The silence felt oppressive, as though the forest was holding its breath, waiting for them to make their next move. The path before them stretched out endlessly, twisting in strange ways, as if mocking their attempts to understand it. And yet, there was a compelling force, something ancient and powerful, drawing them forward.

Selisyn could feel her heart racing in her chest, the rhythm of it pulsing in sync with the song that echoed through the air. It wasn't a melody that could be ignored. No matter how much she tried, she couldn't block it out. The haunting, otherworldly notes wrapped around her like tendrils, pulling her deeper into this place, deeper into the mystery of it all.

Beside her, Thalior was still lost in thought, his jaw clenched as though he were holding onto something—an answer, a realization, anything that would make sense of the chaos around them. His hand was twitching at his side, as though he wanted to reach out to her, but was afraid of what it might mean.

The pull between them was undeniable. Selisyn had felt it the moment they touched. A spark, a connection that had surged through her like a lightning strike. It was as though their souls had recognized each other across time and space. But what did it mean? What was the significance of this connection?

"Do you think we can break it?" she asked, her voice barely a whisper.

Thalior turned to face her, his eyes searching her face, as if he were trying to gauge whether she had the same thoughts, the same fears. "I don't know," he said finally, the words heavy with the weight of uncertainty. "I don't even know what 'breaking the cycle' means. What if we fail?"

She stepped closer to him, the tension in the air between them palpable, but comforting in some strange way. "I don't think we have a choice. We have to try."

His gaze softened, just a fraction, but it was enough. Enough for her to see the trust in his eyes. The same trust she felt growing within her, despite the confusion, despite the danger. The connection was there, undeniable, and in that moment, she realized that it wasn't just the song drawing them together. It was something deeper, something beyond their understanding.

But that didn't make it any less terrifying.

Without a word, Thalior began to walk, his movements steady, as though he had made up his mind. Selisyn followed, her footsteps light on the ground, as though the earth beneath her feet was too fragile to bear her weight. The song, still faint, pulsed in her chest, a constant reminder that they weren't alone in this realm. It was watching them, waiting for them to make their move.

The forest was unchanging, its trees stretching endlessly into the sky. The shadows deepened as they walked, the light growing dimmer with each step. It was disorienting. Nothing felt real here—no sun, no stars, no cycles of day and night. It was a place stuck between worlds, suspended in a moment that never ended.

"How long have you been here?" Selisyn asked, her voice

breaking the silence. "You said... you said you've been wandering."

Thalior glanced over at her, his face shadowed by the darkening forest. "I don't know how long," he admitted. "Time doesn't pass here. Not in the way you'd think. It's like... like you wake up one moment, and the next moment, it's like no time has passed at all. You think you've been here a few days, and then it's been weeks, months, or longer. It plays tricks on your mind."

Selisyn nodded, her thoughts spinning. How could anyone endure this? Trapped in a realm where time didn't exist, where everything was suspended in an endless loop, impossible to escape. She couldn't fathom it. And yet, here they were, standing at the precipice of something far greater than either of them could have anticipated.

As they walked deeper into the forest, the song grew louder again, more urgent. It vibrated through the air, seeming to call out to them, but also to warn them. The deeper they went, the more intense it became, and Selisyn could feel it in her very bones. The pull was getting stronger, drawing them in.

Suddenly, the trees parted, revealing a clearing up ahead. The air shifted, and Selisyn's heart skipped a beat. There, in the center of the clearing, was something that she could not have expected.

A figure. An ancient being, dressed in flowing robes that shimmered with a strange light, like the stars themselves had been woven into the fabric. His eyes were hidden beneath a dark hood, but the power radiating from him was unmistakable. He stood still, watching them with an intensity that made her blood run cold.

Thalior stopped beside her, his posture stiffening as he

recognized the figure. "Vorrin," he said, his voice strained. "You were right… you've been watching us."

The figure nodded slowly, the movement fluid, like he was part of the very air around them. "I have been waiting," Vorrin said, his voice a deep, rumbling echo that seemed to come from everywhere at once. "Waiting for the moment when the two of you would cross the threshold."

Selisyn felt a chill run down her spine. "The threshold?" she repeated, her voice trembling.

Vorrin's hooded eyes turned toward her, and for a moment, it felt as though he could see right through her, into the depths of her soul. "Yes," he said softly. "The threshold into the true nature of your existence. This realm, this place… it was never meant for you. But it is where you are bound, for now. The song… it is not merely a call. It is a test. And you are the ones who must face it."

"Test?" Selisyn's voice was barely a whisper, the word foreign and unsettling. "We didn't ask for this. We didn't ask to be brought here."

"No," Vorrin agreed, his voice tinged with sorrow. "None of us ask for the song. But it chooses its own. And it has chosen you."

Thalior stepped forward, his fists clenched. "What is it, Vorrin? What is the song? Why is it pulling us toward each other?"

Vorrin's lips curved slightly, though it was not a smile, but rather a knowing expression, one that carried with it the weight of centuries. "The song is the melody of eternity itself. It binds souls, intertwining them across time, across worlds. And you, Thalior, Selisyn—you are part of that song. You were always meant to be."

Selisyn's heart pounded in her chest. "But we don't understand. We don't even know why we're here."

Vorrin's gaze softened, just for a moment, before it hardened again. "That is what you must learn. To understand the song, you must first understand the bond between you. Only through that can you break the cycle, and free yourselves."

The air around them seemed to grow thicker, heavier. The song echoed again, louder now, vibrating in the ground beneath their feet. It was everywhere—inside them, around them. It was alive.

"I don't know if we can do this," Selisyn murmured, her voice raw. "I don't even know how."

"You will," Vorrin said, his voice like a promise, deep and unfathomable. "But the journey is not without sacrifice. And the path will not be easy. The song will test you, but it will also guide you. It is both creation and destruction. It is your choice whether to embrace it or reject it."

The last words echoed in the air like a bell tolling, a warning and a call at the same time.

Thalior turned to Selisyn, his expression unreadable. The weight of what Vorrin had said hung between them, a palpable force, and for a moment, neither of them spoke.

Then, with a final, shared glance, they began to walk toward the center of the clearing, where the song swelled to a crescendo. They didn't know what would happen next, but they knew that the path ahead was theirs to choose.

Together.

And no matter the cost, they would face it side by side.

Three

The Song Unfolds

The sunless sky above stretched in shades of violet and gold, casting an eerie glow over the forest. The trees, tall and ancient, whispered secrets in a language lost to time. Their leaves shimmered with an iridescent hue, as though the forest itself was alive, breathing, watching. Every now and then, the wind stirred the branches in a rhythm, matching the distant song that seemed to pulse through the air—a melody that tugged at their hearts, at their very souls.

Selisyn and Thalior stood together on the edge of a glistening river, its waters reflecting the strange colors of the sky. The song had grown louder, more insistent, pulling them closer, as though it had become an extension of their being. It felt as though they could hear the very pulse of it in their veins, in their breaths, a constant hum that threaded their lives together in ways neither of them fully understood.

Since their encounter with Vorrin, the world around them

The Song Unfolds

had shifted. The eternal forest, which had seemed so familiar at first, had begun to change. Where once there had been lush groves and towering oaks, now vast stretches of desert lay before them, the dry, cracked earth reflecting the fiery hues of the sky. The ocean had risen, swallowing the dunes and giving way to tall, jagged mountains, their peaks lost in a mist that glowed faintly, casting shadows that twisted unnaturally. The world was unmoored, as if time had no hold here, and everything was in constant motion—shifting, bending, folding in on itself.

But despite the disorienting changes, there was one constant. The bond between them. Their connection.

Each time they were apart, the song grew quieter, more distant. It became a mere whisper in the back of their minds, something they could almost forget. But when they were together, it thrummed louder, as if the universe itself was aligning, its threads weaving around them. The air crackled with energy, electric and alive, pulling them into one another with an undeniable force.

Selisyn couldn't explain it, but she felt it deep within her—a pull toward him that was as natural as breathing. And though they hadn't spoken the words aloud, she knew he felt it too. The way his eyes lingered on hers, the way his hand brushed against hers when they stood in silence—it was all part of a language they didn't need to speak.

She turned to him now, her fingers grazing his. The touch sent a shiver of warmth down her spine, and her heart raced, quickening in response to the song. "Thalior," she murmured, her voice barely above a whisper, as if speaking louder would shatter the fragile peace between them. "Do you feel it? The song… it's so strong."

He nodded, his expression dark and contemplative. "I do. It's becoming… harder to ignore. I've never felt anything like this before."

He stepped closer to her, his presence a quiet force, and for a moment, the world around them seemed to fade. The sound of the song filled their minds, vibrating through the air like a low hum. The river beside them rippled, and for the briefest of moments, the surface shimmered, casting their reflections back at them, distorted and strange.

Selisyn reached out, her hand trembling slightly as she traced the surface of the water. "It's like everything we do, everything we feel… it's changing this place."

Thalior watched her with an intensity that made her breath catch. "I think it's not just changing this place, Selisyn. It's changing us."

She turned to face him, the weight of his words settling over her like a heavy cloak. He was right. The more time they spent together, the more the world around them seemed to bend and shift. The sunless sky above them darkened further, rippling like liquid as strange, colorful streaks of light twisted through the clouds.

The song rose again, louder now, and it felt almost as if it were becoming something more than just music. It was alive. It was conscious. It was speaking to them, reaching into the very core of their beings, pulling at their hearts in a way that made them ache.

"We have to keep moving," Thalior said, his voice quiet but determined, as if trying to shake off the weight of the atmosphere that surrounded them. "This place… it's changing too fast. I don't like it."

Selisyn nodded, stepping away from the river's edge. Her

pulse quickened, but she forced herself to focus. Whatever was happening, they had to find a way to understand it, to navigate the shifting realm that seemed to be at once beautiful and terrifying.

They began walking again, their footsteps muffled by the soft, ethereal moss beneath their feet. The ground beneath them seemed to shift, the earth almost undulating, as if the forest itself were breathing with them, alive with the rhythm of the song.

As they ventured deeper into the heart of the shifting world, the trees began to thin, and the landscape transformed once again. The once-familiar forest now gave way to a vast, arid plain. The air was dry, crackling with static energy, and the ground was cracked, stretching out into the distance in a sea of dust and shattered stone.

Selisyn squinted against the harsh sunlight, trying to make sense of their surroundings. There were no landmarks, no familiar markers to guide them. It was as if they had stepped into a new world entirely, one that stretched out forever without beginning or end.

The only thing constant was the song. The melody had grown louder now, filling the air around them. It was no longer just a soft hum. It was a crescendo, a deafening, pulsating force that seemed to vibrate in her chest, in her very bones.

And then, as if summoned by their thoughts, a shadow appeared at the edge of their vision. Selisyn froze, her heart skipping a beat. She glanced at Thalior, but his eyes were narrowed, his senses alert. He had felt it too.

A figure, dark and undefined, stood just beyond the edge of their sight. It was as though it had materialized from the air itself, its form flickering in and out of focus. The figure was tall, cloaked in shadows, and as it moved, the very ground seemed to tremble beneath its feet. It was as though the landscape itself recoiled in its presence.

"Who's there?" Selisyn called, her voice stronger now, but the figure did not respond. It merely continued to move in their direction, its form wavering like smoke in the wind.

Thalior's hand instinctively reached for hers, his grip firm and steady. "Stay close," he said, his voice low, filled with a mixture of caution and something else—something darker, something he had yet to share.

The figure drew closer, and now they could see it clearly. It was a woman, her features obscured by the shadows, but her eyes glowed faintly, like embers in the dark. The air around her was thick with a palpable sense of malevolence, a force that made the air feel heavier, suffocating.

"Druvielle," Thalior whispered, his voice barely audible, but filled with recognition. "It's her."

The woman—Druvielle—paused a few paces away from them, her eyes fixed on Selisyn with an intensity that sent a chill running down her spine. She said nothing, but her presence alone was enough to make the song falter, to make the world around them waver.

"Why are you here?" Thalior demanded, his voice edged with both fear and defiance.

Druvielle's lips curved into a faint, knowing smile. "I am here because you called me," she said, her voice like velvet, dark and soft, but carrying with it the weight of something ancient, something unyielding. "I have been watching you both. Waiting."

Selisyn's heart thudded in her chest, a feeling of dread settling over her. She had no idea who this woman was, but

The Song Unfolds

something in the depths of her gaze told her that Druvielle's presence was no coincidence. She was tied to the song, tied to them, in ways they had yet to understand.

"You don't belong here," Selisyn said, trying to steady her voice. "You're not part of this. Leave us alone."

Druvielle's smile deepened, her eyes glimmering with a dangerous light. "Ah, but I am part of this, dear child. I have always been part of it. And so have you."

The world around them seemed to still, the air growing thick with tension. The song, once a harmonious force, now felt discordant, like a melody that had gone off-key. Everything, every part of this strange world, seemed to hinge on the three of them now, their fates entwined in ways neither of them could yet comprehend.

As Druvielle took another step forward, the ground beneath them trembled. The song grew louder, its haunting notes vibrating through the very fabric of the world. The forces at play, the forces of love, time, and fate, had been set in motion, and there would be no turning back.

Druvielle's presence was overwhelming. It wasn't just her figure, cloaked in shadows that seemed to devour the light. It was the air around her, thick with an unsettling energy, that made Selisyn's heart pound faster. The world around them was shifting in ways that defied logic—trees melting into dust, the sky turning to a shade of bruised purple that deepened with every passing moment. Everything seemed to be folding, collapsing, drawn to this one person, this woman who seemed to exist on the edges of reality.

Thalior stepped in front of Selisyn, his hand gripping the hilt of the blade that he had yet to draw, as if the weight of it alone would be enough to protect them from whatever force Druvielle was about to unleash.

"You don't belong here," he repeated, his voice stronger, though the tremor in it betrayed his fear. "Whatever you are, whatever you're trying to do, it ends now."

Druvielle's lips parted in a smile, slow and deliberate, her gaze flicking between Thalior and Selisyn. "Ah, such bravado. But you both don't understand, do you? You are not the ones in control here. The song, this place—it is a force greater than you can imagine."

The world seemed to inhale at her words, the ground shifting again, now trembling beneath their feet. It was as though the very fabric of the realm was alive, responding to her presence, responding to the change she was bringing. Selisyn felt it in her chest, the pressure building up like a storm ready to break.

"Who are you?" Selisyn's voice was steady despite the chaos swirling inside her. She wasn't sure what she expected—some dark sorceress from another age? A trapped spirit, perhaps, cursed to roam the lands forever?

Druvielle's eyes flickered with amusement. "I am neither of those things, dear child. I am a keeper. A warden of the song. And as long as you are here—" She paused, her smile deepening. "As long as *you two* are here, you will learn what it means to exist outside of time. You will learn that the price of love in this place is not what you think."

Selisyn felt the weight of those words settle over her like a blanket of ice. She looked at Thalior, the connection between them stronger than ever, even as the world threatened to fall apart around them. She wanted to reach for him, to hold on to that bond, but something in Druvielle's eyes made her hesitate.

"What are you talking about?" Thalior demanded. His voice

had an edge now, though his eyes flickered with uncertainty. "You said we called you. What do you want?"

Druvielle tilted her head, her eyes narrowing. "You called me, yes. Not in words, but in the very essence of your souls. You two are bound together in ways you cannot comprehend. The song that brought you here, that binds you now, is not simply an echo of time. It is a force—a force that will either tear this place apart or allow it to endure forever."

"Endure forever?" Selisyn repeated, a chill crawling up her spine. "What does that mean?"

Druvielle's smile softened, but it was no less ominous. "It means that your love, as beautiful and as pure as it may be, has consequences. You see, you two are not just trapped in a timeless world. You are the cause of it. The song chose you. Chose you to be its final note, its crescendo. You are the ones who will either break the cycle... or bring it to an end forever."

The air around them crackled, the ground shifting again beneath their feet as the desert stretched out before them, the horizon darkening with each word that left Druvielle's lips.

Selisyn's mind raced. She could feel the pulse of the song, growing stronger with every passing second, resonating deep inside her. It wasn't just a melody. It was an echo of something larger, something ancient, something that had been waiting for them. But what was it? What did it want? And why did they—of all people—have to bear its weight?

Thalior was silent, his gaze never leaving Druvielle, his fingers still curled around the hilt of his blade. There was a resolve in his eyes now, one that Selisyn hadn't seen before. It was as though the fear had faded and been replaced by something else—a quiet understanding that whatever this was, whatever the song had in store for them, it was now too late to turn back.

"We're not going to let you control us," he said, his voice low but unwavering.

Druvielle's gaze darkened, her smile slipping slightly. "Control? No, Thalior. I do not seek control. I merely seek to *guide* you through this. To help you understand your role in the song's unfolding."

"And what is that role?" Selisyn demanded, her voice sharper now. "To die? To be part of some twisted game of fate?"

Druvielle's eyes flashed with a cold, knowing light. "Death is not the end in this place, child. It is merely a transition. A transformation. A merging of your very essence with the eternity you are bound to."

Selisyn felt her breath catch in her throat. *Merging with eternity?* What did that even mean?

The shadows around Druvielle seemed to deepen, swirling as if they were alive, moving with a sentience of their own. And then, as though her presence alone had caused the world to bend in on itself, the ground beneath their feet began to tremble again, this time with greater force. The air was thick with the weight of it, and the sound of the song grew louder, louder until it was all-encompassing. It wasn't just in their heads anymore. It was everywhere, all around them, vibrating the very air.

"You must understand this, both of you," Druvielle said, her voice cutting through the chaos like a blade. "This song, this place, it is not some accident. It is not a mistake. You were chosen to be part of it, whether you like it or not."

She stepped forward, closing the distance between them. The air around her shimmered with a strange, cold energy that made the hairs on the back of Selisyn's neck stand on end.

The Song Unfolds

"You are the beginning and the end, Selisyn and Thalior. You are the song that will either break the cycle or seal it forever. And the price you will pay for this—your love, your bond—it will not be simple. It will cost you more than you can imagine."

The world seemed to warp, twisting into a violent spiral as if the very fabric of time was stretching to its limits. Selisyn felt a cold, dizzying sensation overwhelm her, as though the ground beneath her was shifting out of her control. And through it all, the song pulsed, relentless, carrying her heart along with it, pulling her deeper into its rhythm.

Thalior reached for her hand, his fingers warm and firm, grounding her in the chaos. "We'll find a way out of this," he murmured, his voice steady despite the turmoil around them. "We have to."

But Druvielle's laughter echoed in the air, sharp and cruel. "You cannot escape what is already written. This place—this song—it will always lead you back to the same conclusion."

Selisyn's heart raced as the ground continued to tremble beneath them. The shadows around Druvielle deepened until they enveloped her entirely, leaving only the faint glow of her eyes visible in the darkness. The song had grown so loud now, so powerful, that it drowned out everything else, filling every part of their being with its resonance.

"You are bound to me," Druvielle whispered, her voice low, almost seductive. "Bound to this place. And soon, you will understand why."

Before either of them could respond, the ground beneath their feet cracked wide open, a chasm forming between them and the dark figure before them. The song rang out one final time, a shriek of pure emotion, before everything went silent. And in the stillness, Selisyn felt her heartbeat echo, louder than ever, and the faintest whisper of a memory she had never lived filled her mind, a reminder that nothing—*nothing*—could remain unchanged in a world without time.

Four

The Betrayal:

The moonlight bled through the cracks in the canopy, casting fragmented shadows on the forest floor. The trees twisted and contorted like ancient sentinels, their gnarled limbs reaching toward the heavens. The world, once so steady and real, was now an ever-shifting blur, a dream and nightmare entwined. But it was the dream that haunted Selisyn.

Night after night, the visions came. Not of this world, but of another. A world where time flowed differently—where Selisyn was not the woman she had become but a queen, ruling over a land of vast beauty and unfathomable power. The dreams began simply enough, filled with a sense of grandeur, the throne room bathed in a golden light. But as they unfolded, they darkened, morphing into something far more sinister.

In her dreams, she stood before him—*Thalior*—a man whose eyes burned with ambition, a sorcerer so powerful that even the winds seemed to bow before him. He stood at her side, once her most trusted ally, the man who shared her bed and her heart. But in these dreams, there was a coldness to him, a chilling distance that Selisyn couldn't comprehend. And then it happened. The betrayal.

She saw him standing before a stone altar, his hands raised high in dark incantation. The air crackled with a malevolent energy as the spell he cast tore through the very fabric of their world. She screamed his name, but it was too late. The earth trembled beneath them, the sky darkened, and the world shattered. He had sacrificed her for power, for control. She had died in that moment, her last breath stolen by the very man she loved.

Selisyn awoke in the dead of night, her body trembling with

The Betrayal

the weight of the dream, her heart pounding as if it had been torn asunder. The room was silent except for the soft rustle of the wind through the trees outside. The familiar, soft sound of the Eternal Song hung in the air, soothing yet oppressive. But the melody now felt different, alien even, like it no longer carried the warmth it once did.

The first few nights, she dismissed the dreams as mere figments of her subconscious. But as they grew more vivid, more insistent, she began to question. *Was it a dream? Or was it a memory?*

She turned toward the bed beside her, where Thalior lay asleep, his face peaceful, though his brow was furrowed in the way it always was when he was troubled. A cold shiver ran down her spine as she studied him. The visions, the pull of the song—it all pointed to something greater than they could understand. And she feared that what they shared now might not be enough to withstand the weight of their past.

Thalior awoke with a sharp breath, his eyes wide and panicked, as though he had been caught in a nightmare. His gaze locked with hers, and for a long moment, they said nothing, the unspoken understanding lingering between them. It was as if they were both caught in the same web of uncertainty, unable to escape the snare of their past lives.

"You had the dreams too," she said, her voice barely above a whisper.

He nodded, his eyes shadowed with something darker than mere exhaustion. "Yes. I don't understand them, Selisyn. They... they feel so real, so vivid. I saw myself... *I saw myself betray you.*"

A sickening knot twisted in her gut. "You saw it too?"

He didn't answer right away. Instead, he stared at her as if trying to read her soul, as though searching for something she couldn't name. The silence between them stretched, thick and uncomfortable.

"I don't know what it means," Thalior said at last, his voice strained. "But it wasn't just a dream. It felt... like a warning. A *truth*."

Her breath caught in her throat. The last remnants of the dream still clung to her, like a shadow on the edge of her mind. She couldn't shake the feeling that it wasn't just a vision—it was a memory. Their souls, their love, bound in a cycle that neither of them could break. She could feel it, the connection between them stronger now than it had ever been. But that connection, she feared, was fragile. If the past had any sway over the present, if it was true that they had once been torn apart by betrayal, then was their love truly meant to last?

The sound of the wind outside grew louder, carrying with it a strange, hollow resonance. The song. It called to them both, but this time, it didn't feel like a melody of hope. It felt like a warning, a reminder of the price they might have to pay for the love they shared.

"I can't ignore this," Selisyn said, standing abruptly. "I have to know the truth. I can't keep living with this doubt."

Thalior stood as well, his hand reaching out to stop her. "What are you saying?"

"I'm saying we need answers. The dreams, the song—it's all too much. I can't pretend that this bond between us is enough to ignore what we saw. What if we're destined to repeat the same mistakes? What if this love is doomed from the start?"

Thalior's face paled as he took a step toward her, his hand shaking as he grasped her arm. "You don't believe that. You can't. I don't care what we were before, Selisyn. I care about

The Betrayal:

what we are now. *You* are everything to me. You always have been."

But Selisyn pulled away from him, her eyes filled with a mixture of confusion and pain. "That's the problem, Thalior. How do we know we're not just repeating the same mistakes? How do we know that this isn't a trick—some cruel game of fate?"

Before Thalior could respond, the air shifted, the temperature plummeting. The familiar presence of Druvielle Saelor manifested before them, her dark form materializing from the shadows as if she had been waiting for the perfect moment to appear.

"You're both struggling," Druvielle's voice echoed, smooth and cold as ice. "The past is a dangerous thing to dwell upon. It can cloud your judgment, make you question everything. But sometimes, the past *is* the key to understanding your present."

Thalior stepped forward, his anger rising like a tide. "What do you want, Druvielle? Haven't you already done enough?"

Druvielle's lips curled into a smile, though it was devoid of warmth. "I am here to offer you a solution, Thalior. A way out of your torment."

Selisyn's eyes widened in disbelief. "A solution?"

Druvielle's gaze flicked to Selisyn, then back to Thalior, her eyes gleaming with something she could not name. "You want to break the cycle, don't you? You want to escape this place, to escape the song. I can make that happen, but there is a price. One that requires sacrifice."

Thalior's breath caught in his throat, but his gaze never wavered from Druvielle. "What kind of sacrifice?"

Druvielle's smile widened, her eyes gleaming with a cold, calculating light. "The price for freedom is simple, Thalior.

You must separate from Selisyn. You must choose to leave her behind."

Selisyn felt her heart stop in her chest. "What?" Her voice was barely a whisper. "What do you mean?"

Druvielle stepped closer, her presence overwhelming, pressing in on them both like an oppressive weight. "I am offering you the chance to escape, to break free from this cycle. But you must choose—*her* or freedom. The song will end, but only if you choose to sever the bond between you."

For a long moment, Thalior stood frozen, his eyes flicking between Druvielle and Selisyn. The words hung in the air like a noxious cloud, choking the life from him.

"I don't believe you," he finally spat, his voice hoarse with emotion. "This is a trick. You want to tear us apart. You always have."

Druvielle's smile faltered for a brief moment, but she quickly regained her composure. "You misunderstand me, Thalior. I'm giving you a choice. A choice that will break the cycle. Choose freedom, or choose her. But you cannot have both."

Selisyn felt a wave of nausea wash over her. Her legs buckled beneath her as the weight of Druvielle's words settled in. *Separate from him?* The thought was unbearable.

But Druvielle's voice pierced the silence, sharp as a blade. "You will make your choice soon, Thalior. Time is running out, and the song is only growing stronger. The fate of both of you rests in your hands."

As Druvielle's form dissolved into the air, leaving only the faintest echo of her presence, Selisyn and Thalior were left standing in the silence of the forest, the weight of the decision pressing down upon them like an unshakable force.

And for the first time since they had arrived in this timeless world, Selisyn wondered if the love they shared was truly enough to overcome the shadows of the past.

Thalior stood motionless, his chest rising and falling in slow, deliberate breaths. The lingering echo of Druvielle's words reverberated in the air like a dark melody, vibrating in the very bones of the forest. His eyes, usually so steady and unwavering, now darted around the space, as if searching for an escape that wasn't there.

Selisyn watched him, her heart hammering in her chest. She wanted to reach out to him, to comfort him, to tell him that they would face whatever came next together. But a chasm of doubt had opened between them, one she wasn't sure could be crossed. The love they shared felt as if it were slipping through her fingers like sand, and with each passing second, the weight of Druvielle's offer pressed heavier on them both.

"Thalior," she whispered, her voice trembling as she took a step forward. "Please, don't listen to her. Don't let her tear us apart."

He turned his gaze toward her, his face a storm of conflicting emotions. The pain in his eyes was unmistakable—he didn't want to choose between her and freedom. He didn't want to betray her again. But Druvielle's words had planted a seed of doubt, and now it was taking root, twisting and turning in his mind, suffocating the very trust that had once held them together.

"She's offering us a way out, Selisyn," Thalior said quietly, his voice hoarse. "A chance to break free from this endless cycle."

"*At what cost?*" Selisyn shot back, her voice rising. "You would *choose* to abandon me? After everything we've been through?"

Her words hit him like a blow. His breath caught in his throat as he took a step back, as though her accusation had physically wounded him. He didn't want to choose. He never had. But the weight of the temptation—freedom from this never-ending realm, from the endless song—was too much to ignore.

"You don't understand, Selisyn," Thalior said, his voice strained. "This place, this realm—it's not real. We are not real. It's all a prison. And Druvielle... she has the power to free us."

"But not without a price," Selisyn snapped, her eyes burning with frustration and fear. "She wants us to sacrifice what we are to each other. She wants to tear us apart."

For a long moment, neither of them spoke. The song continued to play, its melody growing louder, more insistent, until it felt like it was inside their heads, reverberating through every thought, every breath. The sound was suffocating, a constant reminder of the forces at play in this place, a reminder that they were trapped in a world where time no longer held any meaning.

"Do you hear it?" Thalior whispered, his eyes distant. "The song is changing."

Selisyn closed her eyes, focusing on the sound. At first, it had been a beautiful thing, a gentle caress that had drawn them together, a beacon in the darkness. But now, it felt darker, heavier—more like a curse than a blessing. The melody had changed, evolving with the tension between them, a reflection of the choice they had to make.

"I hear it," she said softly, her voice barely above a whisper. "It's like it knows what we're about to decide."

Thalior's gaze flicked to her, his eyes filled with uncertainty. "And what if we choose wrong, Selisyn? What if we make the wrong choice, and everything we've fought for—everything we've felt for each other—was in vain?"

The question hung in the air like a lead weight, and Selisyn's heart twisted painfully in her chest. She wanted to deny his fear, to tell him that their love was stronger than any trial or temptation. But the truth was, she didn't know. She didn't know if they could survive the weight of the past, if their love could withstand the betrayal that had once torn them apart.

Suddenly, the air shifted, cold and sharp as though the very atmosphere had been carved by an unseen blade. Selisyn's eyes snapped open, and she saw him—Druvielle. Her figure materialized from the shadows once more, her form flickering like a ghost before solidifying, her eyes gleaming with the cold, calculating intensity that had become her trademark.

"I see you've made your decision," Druvielle said, her voice dripping with mockery. "You can't resist, can you? The temptation of freedom is too much."

"I haven't made any decision yet," Thalior snapped, his tone sharp with frustration. "I'm not going to abandon her, Druvielle."

The figure of Druvielle tilted her head slightly, as though studying him with an unreadable expression. "You misunderstand, Thalior. I'm not asking you to abandon her. I'm offering you a way out. A way to escape the endless cycle of suffering."

Selisyn stepped forward, her hands clenched into fists at her sides. "And you think that *separating* us is the answer?"

Druvielle's lips curled into a sly smile. "Not *separating—freedom*. I offer you both freedom, Thalior. If you choose the path of release, you can leave this place. You can return to the world you once knew."

"And what of Selisyn?" Thalior demanded. "What happens to her?"

The Hollow Song of Eternity

Druvielle's smile widened, her eyes gleaming with dark amusement. "She, too, will be free. But only if you make the choice. Only if you decide that your love is not worth the cost of eternity."

Selisyn felt her breath catch in her throat. "What does that mean? *What cost?*"

Druvielle's eyes flashed with a dangerous gleam. "The cost of eternity is one soul, one heart. You are both tethered to this place, to this realm. But the bonds that bind you can be severed. The choice is yours, Thalior."

Selisyn felt a cold chill spread through her limbs as Druvielle's words sank in. The idea of losing Thalior was unbearable, but the idea of losing herself—to a fate that she could not even begin to understand—was even worse. She had to make him see. She had to make him realize that their love was worth fighting for, that no price, no temptation, was too great.

"Thalior," she said, her voice trembling but resolute, "this is a lie. It's all a lie. If we separate, we lose everything. *You* lose everything. You'll be no better than the sorcerer you once were. The one who betrayed me."

Thalior looked torn, his hands trembling as he reached out for her. His eyes, filled with desperation, locked onto hers. "I don't want to lose you, Selisyn. I don't. But the cost of staying here, of staying trapped in this endless cycle—it's too much. *We* are too much. What if this song, this world, is only holding us back? What if it's all part of a greater trap?"

"You're wrong!" she cried, her voice breaking. "This world may be a trap, but *we* aren't. You aren't. Please don't listen to her, Thalior. Don't let her win."

Thalior stood frozen for a long moment, his eyes locked on hers, and for a moment, Selisyn thought she could see a

The Betrayal:

flicker of understanding in his gaze. But then, his expression hardened, and he turned away from her, his hands clenched into fists at his sides.

"I don't know what to believe anymore," he whispered, his voice low and anguished. "But I know this—I can't lose you again."

As the words left his lips, the forest around them began to shift once more. The trees seemed to tremble, the ground beneath their feet quaking as though the very world was reacting to the choice that had been made. The air thickened, the atmosphere becoming charged with an electric energy that crackled in the space between them.

"You'll regret this," Druvielle's voice echoed, her figure dissolving into the shadows. "You'll regret it all."

Thalior's voice was filled with quiet resolution as he turned back to Selisyn. "No. We won't. Together, we can break the cycle. Together, we can defy fate."

And in that moment, as the world around them seemed to hold its breath, Selisyn realized something—something she had known all along, deep in the recesses of her heart. Their love was not just a bond—it was the key. The key to breaking the cycle. The key to freeing themselves from the song.

As long as they were together, they could withstand anything.

Five

The Heart of the Song

The days bled together, each indistinguishable from the last, as time in the realm grew more distorted, more oppressive. Selisyn could feel the weight of it in every step she took, every breath she drew. There was an ever-growing chasm between her and Thalior, one that she could neither cross nor understand. His eyes, once so full of warmth and certainty, had turned into something distant, like a storm about to break. And though they were together—always together—their bond seemed to fray with every passing moment.

She stood at the edge of a lake, its surface smooth and glassy, reflecting the tumultuous sky above. The faint pulse of the song seemed to vibrate through the very air, a rhythmic thrum that reverberated in her bones. It was a constant, nagging presence, but today, it felt different. There was a sharpness to it, a cruelty. A reminder that they were trapped in a world

The Heart of the Song

where love itself was being twisted into something dark.

Thalior appeared behind her, silent as always, yet his presence made her pulse quicken. She didn't turn to face him. She couldn't. The distance between them was too vast, and she wasn't sure what to say anymore. Words had become useless, incapable of bridging the widening gap.

"I can't," she whispered, her voice barely audible. "I can't keep feeling you slipping away from me."

Thalior said nothing. The sound of his footsteps, the soft scuff of his boots on the earth, was the only indication that he had come closer. She could feel him now, standing just behind her. She had hoped that his touch, his presence, would somehow reassure her, but there was no warmth, no certainty. Only the echo of their shared pain, the weight of their unspoken thoughts pressing down on both of them.

Selisyn finally turned, her eyes locking onto his. The look in his eyes made her stomach churn. He was conflicted, caught in the same storm of confusion and fear that she felt swirling inside her.

"What are we going to do, Thalior?" Her voice cracked, the words tasting bitter on her tongue. "I can't keep losing you like this. I can't keep feeling like we're slipping into nothingness."

His gaze wavered, avoiding hers for a moment before he let out a deep breath, his shoulders slumping under an unseen weight. "I don't know," he said quietly, his voice hoarse with the strain of unspoken grief. "I don't know what to do anymore. Every time I try to grasp onto something solid, it falls away. Every time I think I can save us, the song pulls me back."

Selisyn's heart clenched painfully in her chest. It wasn't enough—this emptiness between them, this growing void that seemed to threaten their very souls. She had known, deep down, that the song was more than just a melody. It was a force, something alive, feeding off their pain, their love, their torment. And it was growing stronger with every moment they allowed it to claim them.

"I can't stand this," she said, her voice now filled with a fierce desperation. "I can't stand knowing that we're trapped in this place, that we're trapped by this… thing. There has to be a way out."

Thalior's gaze darkened, and he stepped closer to her, his fingers brushing against hers in a fleeting touch that sent a shiver of warmth through her. But it was not enough to quell the storm inside her. Not enough to drown out the song that seemed to wrap itself tighter around their hearts with each passing second.

"There is a way," he said, his voice barely above a whisper. "But it's a dangerous one. I've heard whispers of an ancient being, someone who might know the truth behind the song. Fionan Valtor. He's old, older than anything in this realm. They say he knows the secrets of the song, how to break it. How to free us."

Selisyn felt a flicker of hope ignite in her chest, but it was quickly smothered by the crushing weight of doubt. "And if we find him? What happens then? Will he truly help us?"

"I don't know," Thalior admitted, his face drawn with the same uncertainty that had plagued them both since they first stepped into this endless world. "But I can't stand this any longer, Selisyn. I can't keep losing you to this… this thing. We have to try."

For the first time in what felt like forever, Selisyn nodded, a sense of resolution settling over her. "Then we find him," she said, her voice steady despite the fear gnawing at her insides.

The Heart of the Song

"We find Fionan Valtor. And we end this."

The journey to find the ancient being was not an easy one. The realm shifted as they walked, the landscape changing as though it were a reflection of the turmoil inside them. Forests stretched and collapsed into deserts, endless fields of sand rising up to meet the sky, and oceans that reached to the edges of the horizon, their waters dark and ominous. Everywhere they went, the song followed them—an incessant hum, now louder than ever, thrumming in their ears, in their very souls.

Days passed in a blur, each one slipping by in a haze of exhaustion and uncertainty. But the further they traveled, the stronger the song became, its influence over them growing deeper, more insistent. It pulled at them, tugging at their hearts, whispering to them of the power it held—of the power of love and pain, entwined together.

They finally arrived at a place where the song seemed to reach its crescendo, a towering mountain that pierced the sky, its peaks hidden by swirling clouds. It was a place of shadow and light, a place where the very air hummed with a strange energy, thick and charged. And at the base of the mountain stood a cave, its entrance yawning wide like the mouth of some ancient beast, ready to swallow them whole.

"This is it," Thalior said, his voice strained, his gaze fixed on the dark opening ahead. "Fionan Valtor is inside. He has to be."

Selisyn looked up at the mountain, feeling the weight of the journey pressing down on her shoulders. "And if he doesn't have the answers we need?" she asked, her voice barely more than a whisper.

Thalior's eyes met hers, and for the first time in what felt like an eternity, there was a flicker of something solid in his gaze—a glimmer of determination. "Then we'll find another way," he said, his voice steady and sure. "But we can't stop now. Not when we're this close."

Together, they stepped forward, entering the cave. The air inside was thick and heavy, as though the very walls of the mountain were alive, pulsing with energy. The further they walked, the more the song seemed to intensify, vibrating through the stone, through the air, through their very bodies.

And then they found him.

Fionan Valtor stood at the center of the cavern, his form cloaked in shadow. He was ancient—his skin pale and stretched tight over the bones of his face, his eyes glowing with an otherworldly light. He was a figure of power, of ancient knowledge, and of something far darker.

"You've come," he said, his voice a low rumble, like the whisper of a storm. "I've been expecting you."

Selisyn's heart pounded in her chest as she stepped forward, her voice trembling despite her best efforts to remain calm. "You know about the song. The Hollow Song. We need to know how to break it. How to escape this place."

Fionan's eyes gleamed in the dim light, and he studied them both for a long, unsettling moment. Finally, he spoke. "The Hollow Song is a living force, a being that feeds on love and pain, and it grows stronger the more you succumb to it. It has existed for as long as this realm itself. To escape, you must face the Heart of the Song, the entity at the center of this world. Destroy it, and the song will cease to exist."

"But doing so will sever our bond forever," Thalior murmured, his voice barely above a whisper. "Love, as we know it, will be gone."

Fionan nodded. "That is the price of freedom. The Heart of

the Song is the source of your pain, your love, your torment. Destroy it, and you will be free. But you will lose each other in the process."

The words hung in the air like a death sentence. The choice that lay ahead of them was an impossible one, a decision that would change everything.

And yet, Selisyn knew that they had no choice. The song was consuming them, consuming everything they were, and if they didn't act now, they would be lost forever.

"Then we will destroy it," she said, her voice firm. "We will face the Heart of the Song. And we will end this."

But even as the words left her lips, she could feel the song growing louder, its pull stronger, as though it was already preparing for the battle to come.

And in that moment, Selisyn realized that their love was both their greatest strength and their greatest weakness. To survive this, they would have to sacrifice everything they had known—everything they had built.

It was the only way out.

The cavern's oppressive silence swallowed them whole as Fionan Valtor's words echoed in their minds. The weight of the decision pressed down on Selisyn's chest like a stone, threatening to crush her from the inside.

"Destroy the Heart of the Song," she murmured under her breath, almost as though speaking the words aloud would somehow make them more real, more possible. But the more she thought about it, the more the reality of it gripped her— a bond severed forever, love as they knew it wiped from existence.

She turned to Thalior, her heart aching at the sight of him.

The weight of his gaze, the uncertainty, the torment reflected in his eyes mirrored her own. His face was a mask of pain, but beneath it, she could see the same internal struggle that churned in her own soul. He had never been a man to make decisions lightly. But this... this was a decision that would define not just their lives, but their entire existence.

"Thalior," she whispered, reaching out for him. Her fingers brushed his arm, a fleeting touch, but it sent a ripple through the air between them. "Do you understand what this means? Destroying it will tear us apart."

He turned to her then, his hand reaching up to gently cup her cheek. His touch was warm, but it felt distant, as if it were some fragile thing that could shatter with the slightest breeze. "I understand," he said, his voice rough. "I understand that we can't keep living like this, Selisyn. The song is poisoning us. It's twisting everything, making us... making us forget who we really are."

His words hit her like a hammer to the chest. Yes, she could feel it too—the song was no longer just an ethereal hum in the distance. It had become a living, breathing thing that coiled around their hearts, tightening its grip the more they fought it. It was as if it had become a part of them, and without it, they would be lost, untethered.

But could they survive without it? Could they truly live in a world where their love no longer existed? Could they survive a love that was erased, even if it meant they would be free of the curse of this place?

She closed her eyes, feeling the weight of the impossible choice in her chest. The very thought of it made her stomach twist with dread. She loved Thalior—she loved him with every fiber of her being. But did that love outweigh the terror of

The Heart of the Song

what would happen if they severed the bond they shared?

"We don't have a choice, do we?" she said, her voice breaking as she spoke the truth that had been gnawing at her insides since the moment they learned the nature of the song. "It's either we destroy it, or we lose ourselves entirely."

Thalior didn't answer right away. Instead, he studied her face as though searching for something—some glimmer of doubt, some flicker of hesitation. But he found none. She was resolute. She knew what they had to do, even if it tore her heart to pieces.

Finally, he spoke, his voice barely audible. "I'll do whatever it takes to free us, Selisyn. But the thought of losing you… of losing us… it's tearing me apart inside. I can feel it already. The song—it's pulling us into a place where nothing exists but the pain of loving you."

Her heart twisted. She knew. She knew the pain he spoke of all too well. It was a pain that consumed them both, one that they could not escape. The more they tried to fight it, the more it grew.

"Then we fight it," she said, her voice steady despite the storm brewing inside her. "We face the Heart of the Song. We destroy it. And whatever happens after that, we'll face it together."

His eyes searched hers, and for a moment, the world seemed to stand still. The pulsing song faded into the background, and all that remained was the look they shared—raw, vulnerable, and full of love. But it was also filled with a quiet terror that neither of them could escape.

"Together," Thalior whispered, his voice thick with emotion. He leaned down, brushing his lips across hers in a kiss that was soft but laden with the weight of everything they had endured—and everything that was to come.

When they parted, Selisyn's heart felt lighter, but at the same time, heavier. The decision had been made. There was no turning back now. They would go to the Heart of the Song. They would face the entity that had kept them trapped in this cycle for what felt like eternity, and they would destroy it. But it would come at a cost—one that neither of them could fully comprehend yet.

Fionan, who had remained silent through the exchange, finally spoke, his voice ringing out like the tolling of a bell. "The Heart lies at the center of this realm," he said, his eyes narrowing as though he had seen this moment many times before. "But beware. The closer you get to it, the more the song will seek to pull you apart. It feeds on your doubts, your fears, your love. It will twist everything you know. Be prepared for what it may show you."

Selisyn nodded, her gaze hardening with resolve. She would face whatever the Heart threw at her. She had to. They had to.

With Fionan's words echoing in their minds, they left the cavern and began their journey toward the center of the realm. The land around them shifted again, the familiar landscapes distorting into strange, unfamiliar forms. A deep fog rolled in from the horizon, obscuring their path, making it difficult to see what lay ahead. The song was growing louder now, more insistent. It wrapped around them like a tightening noose, its melody shifting from sweet and harmonious to discordant and jagged. Every note seemed to scrape against their skin, pulling at their hearts, and it took all of Selisyn's strength to remain focused.

"Stay close," Thalior whispered, his hand finding hers in the fog. His touch was grounding, but even now, it felt like it was slipping through her fingers. "Don't let go."

The Heart of the Song

Selisyn squeezed his hand, feeling the tremor in his grip. She didn't speak. There were no words left to say. She simply followed him, her eyes fixed on the path ahead, her thoughts filled with a single purpose—reaching the Heart, and ending the song once and for all.

As they pressed forward, the landscape shifted once again, this time into a vast, barren desert. The wind howled around them, carrying with it the scent of decay and something far older than the land itself. The song seemed to fade for a moment, leaving only the eerie silence of the desert.

And then, they saw it.

In the distance, looming before them like a shadow against the dying light of the sky, was the Heart of the Song. It was a massive, pulsating mass of darkness, swirling with colors that did not belong in the natural world—deep violets, glowing reds, and sickly greens, all twisting together in a grotesque dance of light and shadow.

Selisyn's breath caught in her throat. She had expected something dark, something terrifying, but this… this was beyond anything she could have imagined. The Heart was alive, a monstrous thing that seemed to feed off their very presence. She could feel it in the air, the pull of its power, the way it seemed to siphon the life from the world around it.

"We're almost there," Thalior said, his voice strained. "Stay close."

But as they moved toward the Heart, the ground beneath their feet began to tremble. The air grew thick, charged with a malevolent energy that seemed to vibrate through their bones. The song, once distant and comforting, was now a violent roar in their minds, drowning out everything else.

Selisyn's heart raced as she felt a coldness seep into her very soul, a deep, gnawing fear that threatened to overtake her. This was the moment. The Heart was close. The Heart was waiting.

And as they took one final step forward, the ground cracked open beneath them, and they fell into darkness.

Six

The Price of Freedom

The air felt heavier than it ever had before. Each breath Selisyn took seemed to thicken in her chest, as if the very world around her was pressing in, squeezing the life out of her with every exhale. The forest, which had once felt like an eternal refuge, now felt like a prison—each shadow lurking with its own dark secret, every rustling leaf sounding like the whisper of fate.

Thalior was no longer the man she had known. The light in his eyes had dimmed, replaced with a coldness that sent an icy shiver down her spine. She had felt it the moment he had returned from his meeting with Druvielle Saelor—the subtle change that seemed to twist him from within, as if something had been carved out of him, and in its place, an insidious darkness had taken root.

Thalior stood before her now, his back rigid, his jaw clenched as if holding back the roar of a beast within. He was trying to hide it, but Selisyn could see it—the curse was slowly overtaking him, warping his features, making him less human with each passing moment. His skin had paled, his eyes reddened, and the once-lustrous hair that framed his face now seemed to lack its usual vitality, falling limp and lifeless.

Selisyn stepped toward him, the air thick with the tension between them. Her heart was torn in two, the painful ache of betrayal searing through her veins. But still, she couldn't look away. She couldn't leave him. Not when he was so close to being lost forever.

"Thalior," she whispered, her voice breaking as she reached out to him. "What did you do?"

His eyes flickered to hers, but they were empty, distant. "I didn't have a choice, Selisyn. You don't understand what it's like to be offered power... to be promised freedom from this place." His voice trembled, the words coming out as though he were trying to convince himself more than her. "You don't know what it's like to be desperate."

Her fingers brushed against his arm, and she could feel the heat of his skin, but it was a feverish warmth, like the burn of fever that would not subside. The moment her touch made contact with him, she felt the subtle thrum of something malevolent beneath the surface—something that pulsed and shifted like the beating of a heart that was not his own.

"I didn't know," she murmured, trying to steady herself, trying to find the right words, but the anger, the betrayal, clouded her thoughts. "You went to him. You made a deal with Druvielle. You... you promised us to him. And now, look what it's done to you."

Thalior's gaze dropped to the ground, his shoulders trembling as he fought to keep himself together. "I didn't think... I didn't know it would go this far. I thought I could outsmart him. I thought I could control it. But it's..." He shook his head, a hollow laugh escaping his lips. "It's too late. I can feel it changing me. And I'm scared, Selisyn. I'm scared of what I'm becoming."

Selisyn's heart clenched at the sight of him like this—so broken, so consumed by the darkness he had welcomed in, only to realize it had consumed him instead. Her fingers tightened around his arm as if to hold him steady, as if to anchor him back to her. "We'll find a way," she whispered, though doubt gnawed at her from the inside. "We'll fix this, Thalior. We'll undo it. I promise you."

But deep down, a voice whispered that perhaps it was already too late—that there was no going back from the consequences of his actions. She couldn't shake the feeling that the curse was more than just an external affliction—it was tied to him, to the very core of who he was. The price of his deal with Druvielle was far greater than he had ever anticipated.

In the days that followed, Selisyn refused to leave his side, even as the curse took root and began to spread. She searched desperately for answers, for someone who could help them. She had no intention of leaving him to suffer alone, not when the darkness was slowly eroding what remained of his humanity. But the path to a cure was a treacherous one. The more they searched, the more they realized that there were few who could offer help—and even fewer who could be trusted.

And so, it was that they found themselves standing before Ithranos Melaes.

The healer was an enigma, an ancient being who had lived through countless ages, yet his appearance was anything but ancient. He looked young—ageless, even—his long black hair flowing in a cascade down his back, his skin golden and smooth, as though untouched by time. His eyes, however, were ancient, filled with the weight of a thousand lifetimes. His gaze pierced through Selisyn like a knife, seeing far beyond the surface, beyond the fear and desperation that clouded her heart.

"I have heard of your plight," Ithranos said, his voice soft, yet carrying an undeniable weight. He stood in the center of a small clearing, his hands clasped behind his back, his expression inscrutable. "The curse that binds you is not one that can be easily undone. It was not simply a promise made—it was a binding contract forged in the depths of your soul."

Selisyn felt her breath catch in her throat. Every word he spoke only deepened the sense of dread that gnawed at her insides.

"I know what you seek," Ithranos continued, his voice colder now. "You wish to break the curse that now binds your love. But there is a price to pay—a price that you may not be willing to accept."

Thalior, standing beside Selisyn, flinched at the words. His face was pale, his eyes flickering with a mixture of fear and guilt. "What price?" he demanded, his voice tight. "Tell me what I must do. I will do anything."

Ithranos turned his gaze to Thalior, his expression unreadable. "The price is not something you can simply pay with your actions, Thalior. It is a price that touches the very essence of your being. You see, this curse—this pact—is not just a curse of the body. It is a curse of the heart. One of you must give up your ability to love forever in order to break the curse."

Selisyn's heart stopped.

"What do you mean?" she whispered, unable to grasp the full horror of what Ithranos was suggesting.

The Price of Freedom

The healer's eyes flickered between them, his gaze knowing. "In order to break the curse, one of you must sacrifice your ability to feel love. You will become hollow, incapable of ever loving again. The connection you share, the bond that was forged through this realm, will be severed. And you will no longer be able to love each other—or anyone, ever again."

Thalior's breath caught in his throat. "No," he said, shaking his head. "There must be another way. There has to be another way."

Ithranos's expression softened for the briefest moment, but his words remained firm. "There is no other way, Thalior. The curse cannot be undone without a sacrifice. If you wish to be free, one of you must make that sacrifice."

Selisyn felt the ground shift beneath her. The weight of the decision pressed down on her like an invisible force, crushing the air from her lungs. She looked at Thalior, her heart breaking with the knowledge of what this meant. She had never imagined that love, their love, could come at such a cost. But here it was—an impossible choice that they had to make, and no matter what they chose, the pain would be unbearable.

Her voice came out in a whisper, trembling with emotion. "One of us must lose our ability to love... forever?"

Ithranos nodded solemnly. "Yes. It is the only way."

Silence hung in the air, thick and suffocating. Selisyn turned to Thalior, her heart aching with the impossible weight of the decision they now faced. The love they shared, the bond that had been forged between them, was the one thing that had kept them alive in this realm. But if one of them had to give up that love, would it be worth it? Could they truly live in a world where love no longer existed for them?

Thalior's eyes locked with hers, a silent understanding

passing between them. They had come so far together—endured so much—but this… this was beyond anything either of them could have anticipated.

It was a decision neither of them was ready to make. Not yet.

But the time was coming when they would have to choose.

The silence between them was suffocating, each passing moment stretched taut with the weight of their impossible decision. Selisyn could feel her heart racing, her chest tight with a mixture of dread and sorrow. The air seemed to hum with the energy of the curse, as though it too was aware of the price they were being asked to pay. The forest around them, once vibrant with life, now felt dead—its muted colors a reflection of the emptiness that had begun to fill her soul.

She looked at Thalior, her gaze searching his face for some hint of the man she had once known. The man she had loved. But the transformation was undeniable. The curse had begun to alter him in ways that went beyond the physical—the darkness in his eyes, the way his movements had grown stiff, mechanical. It was as if the very act of his betrayal, the pact he had made with Druvielle Saelor, had already begun to eat away at his humanity, leaving a hollow shell behind.

Thalior's eyes were locked on Ithranos, but there was a distant look in them, a coldness that seemed to grow with every word the healer spoke. His hand clenched into a fist at his side, as if he were trying to hold onto something, anything, to keep himself from falling apart.

"I can't lose you," he muttered under his breath, but it was clear that he wasn't speaking to Ithranos, nor to Selisyn. He was speaking to himself. A plea, a confession, perhaps.

Selisyn's heart ached as she stepped closer to him, her fingers brushing against the side of his arm. The connection between them sparked—a fleeting moment of warmth in the coldness that had overtaken him. But even that small comfort was fleeting, as if the bond they had shared was slipping through her fingers like sand.

"I can't lose you, either," she whispered, her voice trembling with unshed tears. "But Thalior... do you understand what Ithranos is saying? One of us must lose our ability to love... forever."

He looked at her then, his eyes filled with anguish, a mixture of guilt and fear. "I know," he said, his voice hoarse. "I know what it means. I..." He hesitated, his breath coming in shallow gasps. "I never wanted this. I never thought it would come to this. But it has. And now we're trapped by it."

The words lingered in the air, each one heavier than the last. Selisyn could feel the tension building between them, a fracture line splitting them apart even as they stood together. She wanted to reach for him, to pull him close, to tell him that they would find another way—that they would fight the darkness together. But the truth was, there was no other way. Ithranos had made it clear. The curse could only be broken with a sacrifice, and that sacrifice would change them both, forever.

Selisyn turned away from Thalior for a moment, her eyes scanning the clearing around them. The world seemed to stretch and shift with an eerie quiet, the trees standing as silent witnesses to their turmoil. The weight of their dilemma pressed down on her, suffocating her. She could feel the pull of the song in her chest, faint but unmistakable—a reminder of the bond that had tied her to Thalior, the bond that had once been so pure, so full of promise. But now it was laced with poison, and the very essence of their love had become a weapon.

She clenched her fists at her sides, trying to steady herself, to push back the rising tide of panic. The thought of losing Thalior—of losing their love—was unbearable. It was as if everything she had fought for, everything they had shared, was slipping away, and she couldn't hold onto it.

"I don't want to lose you," she said again, this time more forcefully, her voice rising in desperation. "But I can't live without love, Thalior. I can't…"

Thalior's face twisted in agony as he reached out for her, his hands trembling. "Please, Selisyn, don't say that. Don't make this harder than it already is."

"I'm not the one who made this choice," she snapped, her emotions unraveling with the weight of the curse pressing on them both. "You did, Thalior. You chose this path. You made that deal with Druvielle. You made the decision that brought us here."

Her words hit him like a physical blow. He staggered back, his hand clutching his chest as if she had pierced him with her words. "I didn't know it would come to this," he whispered, his voice barely audible. "I never wanted to hurt you, Selisyn. I never wanted any of this. I thought I could protect you, that I could make everything right. But I've made it worse."

Selisyn's heart shattered at the raw pain in his voice. She wanted to scream, to lash out, to say all the things she was thinking—the hurt, the betrayal, the hopelessness—but none of it would change anything. She couldn't undo what had been done. They were both trapped in a web of their own making, and the only way out was a decision that would tear them apart.

Ithranos's voice broke through the storm of their emotions, cold and unyielding. "You are not the first to face such a choice," he said, his words carrying the weight of untold centuries. "There have been others who have sought to break the curse, who have come before you, driven by the same desire for freedom. But none of them have succeeded in breaking it without paying the price. Love, as you know it, cannot be restored once it is severed. You must understand the gravity of this decision."

Thalior turned to face Ithranos, his expression hardening. "What if we choose not to break the curse? What if we leave it as it is and continue living with it?"

Ithranos shook his head slowly, his eyes filled with sorrow. "Then you will live as shadows, forever bound to this realm. The curse will consume you both, warping you further until you no longer recognize yourselves. You will be nothing more than vessels for the song—a song that will never stop, never let you go. Your love will wither away, as will your souls."

Selisyn felt her stomach churn at the thought of that fate. A lifetime of hollow existence, a lifetime of living in a world that was not their own, where love was a fleeting dream that would never come to fruition. It was a fate worse than death.

"And if we choose to break it?" she asked, her voice small, almost fragile.

"Then one of you must sacrifice the very thing that defines you," Ithranos replied. "The love that binds you will be severed, and one of you will no longer be able to feel it. The bond you share will disappear, and neither of you will ever know the depth of that love again."

Selisyn could feel the tears welling in her eyes, but she fought to keep them at bay. She wouldn't let herself break. Not yet. Not until they made their choice.

Thalior's voice was thick with emotion as he turned to face her. "Selisyn, I—I don't want to lose you. But I can't ask you to give up your ability to love, to feel everything we've shared. I couldn't live with myself if I took that from you."

"And I can't live without love, Thalior," she whispered, her voice breaking. "I don't know how to exist without it. Without *you*."

For a moment, they stood there in silence, the weight of their decision pressing down on them like a heavy stone. Neither of them knew how to choose. Neither of them could imagine a world without the other.

But the reality was clear. One of them had to make the sacrifice.

The decision loomed over them, the cost of their freedom greater than either of them had imagined.

And in the silence that followed, the sound of the song grew louder, more urgent—its haunting melody a reminder that time was running out, that the heart of the song was drawing nearer, and with it, the end of everything they had known.

Seven

The Shadows That Hunt

The forest was alive, but not in the way Selisyn remembered. The leaves rustled, but the sound was hollow, like the breath of a long-dead creature trying to whisper something forbidden. The air hung thick with an oppressive heat, the kind that made the skin sweat but left the soul feeling frozen. It wasn't the heat of summer or the warmth of a fire, but something darker—something that crept under her skin and made her heart race with anxiety.

Selisyn stood at the edge of a clearing, her fingers gripping the gnarled tree that stood before her like a silent sentinel, watching. She could feel it now—the tension, the unease that had been growing ever since they had made their choice to try and break the curse. The silence was deafening, each breath she took filled with a sense of foreboding. Something was coming. Something that had been lying in wait for them, patient and predatory.

Thalior stood beside her, his posture tense, his eyes darting through the shadows of the forest as though searching for something—or someone. He hadn't said a word since they had entered the clearing, but she could feel the unease radiating from him, a reflection of her own.

"I don't like this," she whispered, her voice barely audible over the crackling of distant thunder.

"I don't either," Thalior replied, his voice strained, as if the weight of their situation had become too much for him to carry alone. "But we've come this far. We can't turn back now."

She glanced at him, her heart twisting at the sight of him. He had always been her rock—the one who held them together, the one whose presence calmed her. But now... now there was a hollowness in his gaze, an emptiness that mirrored the void that had begun to settle in her own chest.

"We've made the right choice, haven't we?" Selisyn asked, her voice trembling slightly, betraying her doubt. "I... I don't know anymore, Thalior. Every step we take, it feels like we're getting closer to something we can't escape from."

Thalior opened his mouth to respond, but the words never came. Instead, his eyes widened in shock, and he stepped back, his hand outstretched as if to shield her from something unseen.

Selisyn turned, but before she could see what had made him react, the ground beneath her feet shuddered. A low growl echoed from the shadows, sending a cold shiver down her spine. Her heart skipped a beat as a figure emerged from the darkened trees.

It was a creature—a shape, half-human, half-beast, cloaked in shifting shadows. Its form was a silhouette, constantly changing, like a nightmare taking shape, its edges rippling and undulating like smoke. But what struck her most were its eyes—black as the void, hollow and cold, staring right through her as though it knew her deepest fears.

Another growl, louder this time, and the creature stepped forward, its claws scraping against the earth. Selisyn instinctively stepped closer to Thalior, the primal need to protect him rising within her. But as she did, she felt a chill run through her veins—a coldness that spread from her chest, wrapping around her heart.

"Selisyn…" Thalior's voice was a low rasp. "Don't look into its eyes."

She looked up at him, confused. "What?"

"Don't… look into its eyes." His voice was urgent now, his hand reaching for her, but it was too late. Her gaze had already locked onto the creature's.

The moment their eyes met, a flood of images exploded into her mind. Past lives—endless cycles of betrayal and loss—each vision more vivid than the last. She saw Thalior, not as he was now, but as something else. A shadow of a man who had once betrayed her, a sorcerer who had abandoned her to the darkness. The memories came crashing in, a tidal wave of pain and regret. The faces of those they had once been—king and queen, lovers, enemies, friends—each one twisted by the choices they had made, each one broken by the curse they could never escape.

And at the center of it all, she saw herself—frozen in time, her heart shattered into countless pieces, each fragment echoing the same refrain: You cannot escape what you have become.

She blinked, and the vision shattered. The world around her spun, the clearing blurring as though she were seeing through a veil of water. She stumbled, her legs weak beneath her, as the creature's form loomed ever closer.

Thalior was there, pulling her back, his hands gripping her arms, his voice hoarse. "Selisyn! Look away!"

But it was too late. The creature's influence was already digging its claws into her mind, pulling her deeper into the darkness. She could feel the weight of it, the crushing pressure of every doubt and fear she had ever buried. It fed on her pain, feeding on her own insecurities, and she could no longer tell where she ended and the creature began.

The growl grew louder, more insistent, as the creature advanced, but Thalior was there—his presence a lifeline in the suffocating darkness. He pulled her into his arms, shaking her, desperate to break her free from the creature's grip. "Selisyn, focus on me. You have to fight it!"

But the pull of the shadows was too strong. She could hear it now—the song, the hollow tune that had haunted them since the beginning. It was all around them, vibrating through the ground, through the air, through their very bones. The creature's form flickered, and Selisyn realized that it wasn't just a monster. It was a manifestation of everything they had been running from. A reflection of their past selves, of their regrets, of the things they had yet to confront.

Thalior's voice broke through the noise, urgent and fierce. "Selisyn, listen to me. Look at me! We're stronger than this. We've faced worse than this."

Her vision cleared for a moment, and she saw him—his face, strained with the weight of their shared torment. His hands cupped her face, his touch warm against her cold skin. She could see the love in his eyes, but beneath that love, she could also see the pain—the guilt that he had never been able to escape.

And that was it. The key. She had to confront her own fears, too. She had to face the darkness that had been haunting her—the fear that their love was doomed, that they were nothing more than pawns in a game they could never win.

She breathed deeply, letting the sound of his voice anchor her. "I'm not afraid of you," she whispered, her voice shaky but resolute. "I won't let you control me."

Thalior's eyes softened as he held her, his strength a steady force against the storm of their emotions. Together, they stood against the creature, their combined will breaking through the grip of its influence.

The creature roared, its form flickering violently, as if struggling to maintain its hold. With a final, desperate cry, it lunged toward them—but in that moment, Thalior raised his hand, his power surging through the air. He shouted something, a word that Selisyn could not understand, but the force of it was enough to send the creature stumbling backward.

The shadows writhed and screamed, but in the end, they faded, retreating into the darkness from which they had emerged.

Selisyn collapsed into Thalior's arms, breathless, her heart still pounding from the encounter. The world around them seemed to breathe a collective sigh of relief, but even in the aftermath of the battle, there was no peace. The air still felt thick with the remnants of the shadow's presence, and the song in the distance grew louder, more insistent.

Thalior held her tightly, his grip tightening as if afraid she might slip away. His body trembled with exhaustion, but he didn't let go. "It's not over, Selisyn," he whispered, his voice ragged. "The shadows will come again. And next time… they won't be alone."

The dread that had taken root in her chest spread further, curling around her heart. She could feel it now—the darkness that had always been there, waiting. And no matter how many shadows they faced, it would always be there, hunting them.

The battle may have been won, but the war was far from over.

The sky had dimmed, though no sun set to bring on the night. The world around them remained caught in a twilight that stretched endlessly, as if time itself had been suspended. The unsettling silence had returned, the air now heavy with the remnants of their battle. Every gust of wind felt like a sigh from the realm, its breath full of sorrow and anticipation.

Selisyn leaned heavily against Thalior, her legs unsteady, though she felt the warmth of his body against hers. She had been shaken, yes, but there was something more terrifying than the shadows they had faced. It was the dread of the unknown—the certainty that they weren't free, not by a long shot.

Thalior's hand rested on her waist, a constant reminder of their bond. His touch was firm, grounding her in the storm of emotions that still whirled within her. But even in his strength, she sensed the tremor beneath his skin—the lingering exhaustion from the battle, and something else. Something darker, more dangerous.

"I don't know if I can do this anymore," she murmured, her voice fragile. The words came out in a ragged breath, as if the weight of them had built up over time and now broke free in a quiet outpouring.

Thalior stiffened beside her, his eyes flickering toward the ground, then back to her, a flicker of pain crossing his face.

The Shadows That Hunt

"You're not alone in this, Selisyn."

Her heart twisted at the sincerity in his voice. He meant it, she knew that. But even his strength seemed not enough against the forces that sought to tear them apart. The bond that had once felt unbreakable now felt like a shackle. The shadows had only been a manifestation of their inner turmoil, a reflection of their fears. What came next?

"I'm so tired, Thalior," she whispered, her words breaking like glass, sharp and aching. "I don't know how much longer I can fight against this—against the past... against what's coming."

The weight of his touch grew heavier, not with burden, but with the quiet promise of solidarity. "Then we'll rest," he said, his voice calm, though she could hear the undercurrent of resolve. "But not yet. Not until we find the answers we need."

He was right. They could not stop now. Not when the shadows had shown them the depth of their wounds. Not when the path ahead was still clouded in the dark mist of their shared fate.

But Selisyn couldn't shake the feeling that something was closing in on them. Something more terrifying than the creatures they had faced, more insidious than the creeping shadows. The song. It had always been there, lurking in the background, but now, it was louder—closer. She could feel it vibrating through her bones, pulling at the edges of her consciousness.

"Thalior," she began, her voice trembling, "the song... it's growing stronger. I can feel it. I don't think it's just the realm anymore."

He turned to her, his face drawn in a mix of concern and determination. "I know," he said, his voice low. "It's not just

The Hollow Song of Eternity

the realm, Selisyn. It's something else. Something tied to us."

The realization was like a blow to her chest. She hadn't voiced the thought aloud, but now that he had spoken it, the weight of it settled heavily on her heart. The song. The hollow, echoing melody that had haunted their every step. It wasn't just a force of nature, wasn't just a cruel reminder of their fate—it was alive. It had a mind of its own. And worse, it was feeding on them.

"The Heart of the Song," Selisyn murmured, her voice barely a whisper as the dread she had been trying to push away crept into her thoughts once again. "The one Fionan spoke of. It's not just an entity. It's a force. A living force that we can't escape. And if we do… the price…"

She trailed off, her words hanging in the thick air between them. The price.

It was a choice she hadn't wanted to make, but the more she thought of it, the more she felt the inevitability of it. They had been warned. Fionan had spoken the truth, though they hadn't fully understood the gravity of his words at the time. The Heart of the Song would give them a way out, a way to end the cycle. But in doing so, they would sever their bond forever.

Selisyn closed her eyes, the thought of it gnawing at her, sinking into her like a poison. To save each other, they would have to destroy the very thing that made them who they were—their love.

"Do you ever wonder, Thalior," she whispered, "if we've already made the choice?"

The words left her mouth before she could stop them, but as soon as they did, she regretted them. They felt like a confession, a hidden truth she had been too afraid to admit until now. The idea that they might already be bound to this fate, that there was no way out—she hadn't wanted to face it. But deep down, she feared it. The shadows they faced were not just physical. They were reflections of their greatest fears—fears that this love, this bond between them, was nothing more than another prison.

Thalior's grip on her tightened, and for a moment, he didn't speak. His silence was heavier than words. She could feel him searching for something to say, something that would reassure her, but nothing came. Instead, he reached into the folds of his cloak, pulling out a small vial of dark liquid. The glow from the forest seemed to bend toward it, as if drawn to its power. The vial shimmered with an ethereal light, pulsing faintly in the dimming twilight.

"Ithranos gave me this," Thalior said softly, his voice full of hesitation. "It's supposed to help. To heal the curse. But there's a catch."

Selisyn turned to him, confusion clouding her thoughts. "What's in it? What's the catch?"

"The catch…" Thalior hesitated again, his brow furrowed in deep thought. "It's not just a cure. It's a test. To break the curse, one of us has to drink it. But the price is… our ability to love."

A chill settled in Selisyn's chest. The weight of his words hit her like a hammer, her breath catching in her throat. "What do you mean, 'our ability to love'?"

Thalior's eyes were filled with sorrow, his voice barely above a whisper. "One of us has to lose the ability to love—to feel love—forever. If I drink it, I won't be able to love you. If you drink it, you'll never be able to love again."

The reality of the choice before them settled heavily in the space between them. The air around them, thick with the scent of earth and magic, seemed to tighten. The world outside the forest—the vast, unknowable expanse of the realm—felt farther away than it had ever been.

"You're asking me to choose…" Selisyn's voice was barely audible, the words falling heavy and thick. "You're asking me to choose between my love for you and your love for me. To take away what's the only thing that's kept us sane in this place."

Thalior's eyes searched her face, his gaze filled with a mixture of regret and determination. "I don't want to lose you, Selisyn. I can't bear the thought of living without you. But I can't live with myself if I let you give up everything just to save me."

There it was—the truth, laid bare in the open. The cruelest choice of all. One of them would have to sacrifice their love, the very thing that bound them, to save the other. It was the ultimate test. The ultimate price.

And in the silence that followed, neither of them spoke. Neither of them moved. The song in the distance continued to hum, and the shadows that haunted them seemed to wait, patient and silent, watching, waiting for them to make their decision.

Eight

The Fire of Doubt

The days blurred together as Selisyn drifted in and out of sleep. She could feel the weight of the realm pressing on her chest, suffocating her in its strange, unyielding embrace. The ethereal trees of the twilight forest whispered constantly, their leaves brushing together in a chorus that spoke of things she couldn't quite understand. Dreams, or perhaps memories, filled her nights—dreams of a queen, a past life too vivid to be simply imagined. The dreams were never gentle. They were sharp, full of anguish, betrayal, and the harshest kind of regret.

And in every dream, she saw Thalior. But he was not the man she loved. No. He was the sorcerer who had destroyed her, the one who had turned away from her in her hour of need. It was as though she were trapped in a world of paradoxes—her love for him twisted into something that felt dangerous, something she could not hold onto without drowning in its depths.

She sat on the edge of a rocky outcrop, gazing out over the endless expanse of the Twilight Realm, its foggy expanse a blur of silver and violet. The distant echoes of the hollow song, once so hauntingly familiar, seemed now like a distant hum that taunted her from afar, reminding her of the impossible choices that lay ahead.

Her fingers brushed the smooth stone beneath her, the surface cool against her skin. She had always found comfort in the feel of stone, the solidness of it beneath her touch. But today, even the stone felt foreign, as though it no longer connected her to the world she had once known.

"Selisyn?"

She turned, her heart leaping as she saw Thalior approaching. He looked different. Not in the way that a change of clothes or time would alter him, but something deeper, something that spoke of the weight of his own burdens. He was as much a prisoner of the past as she was—trapped in a cycle they both struggled to break.

"You're awake," he said softly, his voice edged with worry. He closed the distance between them, standing just a few feet away. His gaze never left her, though he seemed hesitant to approach further.

"I'm awake," she replied, her voice quiet. There was a strained tension in her words, as though each syllable were a careful step over a treacherous cliff. "Though I'm not sure I want to be."

Thalior frowned, his brows knitting together in concern. "What do you mean?"

Her gaze met his, but she couldn't bring herself to fully meet the warmth in his eyes. Instead, she looked past him, her mind searching for something that wasn't there. "I don't know anymore, Thalior. I… I keep seeing her. The queen. In my dreams. And I can't shake the feeling that this… this love between us isn't the way it's supposed to be."

Thalior's expression softened, his hand reaching out in a gesture that was both tender and uncertain. "It's the past, Selisyn. It's the song. It's all part of what's been woven into our fates. You're not the queen. You're not that person anymore."

"But what if I am?" she asked, the words tumbling out before she could stop them. "What if that's why we're here, why we're stuck in this cycle? Maybe I was never meant to trust you, Thalior. Maybe I was always supposed to be this broken person, caught in the web of our past."

The silence between them felt thick, almost suffocating, as the truth of her words hung heavy in the air. It wasn't just the dream that troubled her anymore—it was the fear that her entire existence had been a lie, a twisted echo of a past that had never let go of her.

Thalior's steps were slow as he moved closer, his voice low and filled with urgency. "Selisyn, look at me. You have to know that the past doesn't define us. It never has. What happened to the queen—what happened to us in that life—doesn't have to happen again. I know I made mistakes. I know I hurt you. But we've already faced those demons. Together."

"I don't know if I can believe that," she whispered, her hands trembling as they clenched into fists. "What if I can't trust you this time? What if I'm repeating the same mistakes as her—trusting you when I shouldn't?"

Thalior's face hardened for the briefest moment, a flicker of pain flashing across his features. But then, with a deep breath, he softened. His hand found hers, gently uncurling her fingers and pulling her into a tight embrace.

"I don't expect you to forgive me, Selisyn," he said, his voice quiet, almost a plea. "But I want to show you that I can be the man you need me to be. I'm not the sorcerer from the past. I'm not the one who betrayed you."

His words were like a balm to her wounds, soothing the jagged edges of her broken heart. But there was something more—something she could feel but couldn't quite grasp. She could feel the weight of the past pressing down on them both, a constant, invisible force. She could hear the song now, louder than before, its haunting melody threading through the cracks in her thoughts, demanding attention.

"I'm afraid," she said, her voice barely a whisper, but laden with the heavy weight of her fear. "I'm afraid that this… this love is never going to be enough to save us. That no matter how much we fight against the song, we'll always be trapped."

Thalior pulled back slightly, his hands cupping her face as he searched her eyes. "We're not trapped, Selisyn. I swear to you, we're not. But you need to believe in us. In what we've built together."

Her gaze flickered away, and she shook her head. "How can I? When all I see is a broken reflection of the past? When I'm haunted by the queen's fate? How can I trust in us when I know what happened to her?"

A shadow of doubt clouded Thalior's features, his eyes flickering with something that she couldn't quite decipher. "What do you mean? What have you learned, Selisyn?"

She hesitated, the words weighing heavy on her tongue. The knowledge she had gleaned from Maelithra Daryon, the ancient scholar they had sought for answers, was still too fresh in her mind, too painful to fully process.

"The queen's downfall," Selisyn began, her voice trembling

The Fire of Doubt

with the knowledge she had uncovered, "it was because of her inability to trust you. She couldn't believe in you—she couldn't believe in what you had offered. And it destroyed her. And now… now I wonder if I'm following the same path."

Thalior's expression shifted, his brows furrowing in confusion and concern. "What are you saying? That because of some mistake in the past, we're doomed to repeat it?"

Selisyn nodded slowly, her heart aching with the weight of her own realization. "I'm saying that maybe I'm not capable of trusting you, Thalior. Maybe I'm destined to make the same mistake as her."

The silence that followed felt thick and suffocating, a storm brewing on the horizon of their fragile bond. Thalior's grip on her face tightened, but there was an edge to it now, an underlying tension that hadn't been there before. He seemed to struggle with something, a truth he didn't want to admit, or perhaps a truth he feared.

"I won't lose you to this, Selisyn," he said, his voice fierce with the kind of resolve she had always admired. "I know I've made mistakes. And I can't change what happened in the past. But I will do everything in my power to make you see that I'm not that man. I'm not the one who betrayed you. Not this time."

Selisyn stared into his eyes, searching for any sign of the man she had fallen in love with. But all she saw was the echo of the past—a reflection of the same doubts she carried in her own heart.

"I wish I could believe that," she said softly, pulling away from him, her heart aching with the enormity of the decision she had yet to make. "But I'm not sure I can anymore."

And as the words hung between them, the silence deepened,

thick and unyielding, like the weight of an inevitable storm. The fire of doubt had been lit between them, and it was burning hotter than ever.

The silence stretched between them, as heavy as the air before a storm. Selisyn's heart hammered in her chest, each beat a reminder of the gulf that seemed to be widening between them. She couldn't bear to look at Thalior, yet she couldn't tear her gaze away. His words echoed in her mind, but they did nothing to quell the deep, gnawing fear that had taken root in her soul.

Thalior stood motionless, his expression unreadable. For a moment, he appeared like a stranger—like the man from her dreams, the one who had betrayed her so completely. The one who had caused her pain she could not erase. But even as she thought that, another part of her—somewhere deep inside— longed to reach out to him, to remember who he really was. But fear held her back, and she wasn't sure whether it was the fear of the past, of repeating the mistakes, or something even more terrifying: the fear that she didn't know who she was anymore.

"I... I need time," she said softly, breaking the silence at last. Her voice trembled, betraying the strength she had tried to summon. "I need to think. To understand what's real and what's not. I need to know what's in my heart."

Thalior's jaw tightened at her words, but his eyes softened, sorrow flickering behind them. "I can't give you time, Selisyn. We don't have it. Not with the song, not with everything that's been set in motion. If we don't act soon, everything will be lost—again."

His words struck her like a physical blow, the weight of them pushing down on her chest, suffocating her. She closed her eyes, willing herself not to succumb to the tears that threatened to fall. She could feel the weight of the realm around them, pressing in as if it were alive, feeding off their anguish, twisting it into something darker.

"You're right," she said, her voice low, steadying herself. "We don't have time. But I don't know what to do. I don't know what to feel anymore, Thalior."

There was a long, heavy pause. She didn't look at him, but she could feel him standing there, close enough that his presence was a constant ache in her chest. She felt his anguish, his own confusion and turmoil. And yet, it wasn't enough. Not anymore.

Finally, after what seemed like an eternity, Thalior spoke. His voice was softer now, a quiet whisper that seemed to tremble in the still air. "You feel it too, don't you? The distance. It's there between us, like an invisible wall that grows taller with each passing moment."

Selisyn's heart clenched. She had known it, too. She had felt the invisible gap widening with every strained conversation, every fleeting touch. It was as though something was slipping away from them both, and she didn't know how to stop it. "I don't want it to be like this," she whispered, her voice breaking. "I don't want us to fall apart again. But I don't know how to stop it."

Thalior's hand moved then, slowly, cautiously, and he reached out for her. His fingers brushed her arm, his touch light and tentative. "I never wanted to hurt you. I never wanted to lose you. But I can't make you love me, Selisyn. I can only show you that I'm here. That I'm trying. I'll keep trying, no matter how many times you push me away."

Her breath caught in her throat as she felt the heat of his

touch, the warmth that had always been her anchor. She wanted to melt into him, to let herself be held in the way he had once held her. But a part of her was terrified that if she did, she would be lost. Forever caught in a loop of broken promises and shattered trust.

"Thalior," she began, her voice trembling with the weight of her uncertainty, "I'm afraid I can't trust you again. I'm afraid that no matter how much we want this… we're doomed to fail."

He stiffened at her words, and she saw the hurt flash across his face. But there was no anger, no bitterness—only a deep, raw sorrow. He stepped back slightly, as though her words had physically hurt him, and she felt a sharp pang of regret in her chest.

"I understand," he said softly, his voice strained. "But please, Selisyn… don't give up on us. Not yet."

She met his eyes then, and for a moment, everything else seemed to fade away. The darkness of the realm, the swirling song in the air, the fears and doubts that clouded her heart—they all disappeared in that instant. All that remained was Thalior. His eyes, deep with longing and pain, and the bond between them that still pulsed with a steady, if fragile, rhythm.

"I'm not giving up on us," she said, her voice firm now, though she could feel the tremble in her hands. "But I don't know how to go forward. I don't know how to fix what's broken."

Thalior didn't respond right away. Instead, he just stood there, staring at her as though searching for something within her that he couldn't find. After a long, uncomfortable pause, he spoke again, his voice low and filled with an edge of finality. "We may not have the answers, but we can't let this be the end. We've come too far. And I… I refuse to lose you. Not when I can still feel the truth of us, somewhere inside."

The Fire of Doubt

Selisyn swallowed, the words caught in her throat. The truth of them, the way they still managed to reach each other despite the pain—they were undeniable. But could she trust it? Could she trust him again? She wasn't sure.

"We have to find a way," she whispered, more to herself than to him. "We have to find the way out of this cycle, Thalior. Because if we don't... if we fail, then it will all be for nothing."

"I know," he said softly, his voice full of determination. "And we will. We'll find a way. Together."

The air between them seemed to shift, growing heavier, charged with a new tension. The weight of their shared past, their shared pain, and the uncertainty of what the future held for them pressed down on them both. But beneath it all, there was something else—something fragile, something worth fighting for.

For a moment, they stood in silence, neither of them knowing what to say next. The wind rustled through the trees, carrying with it the faintest notes of the hollow song, a reminder of the ever-present danger that lay ahead. But for a brief, fleeting moment, the world seemed to hold its breath, as though waiting for them to make the choice that would shape their fate.

"I don't know what the future holds," Selisyn said at last, her voice barely above a whisper. "But I know that I want to find out with you."

Thalior's eyes softened as he stepped closer to her, his hand brushing the side of her cheek. "Then we'll face it together. No matter what."

For the first time in days, Selisyn felt a spark of hope flicker in her chest. It was small, fragile, but it was enough to remind her of what she had once believed: that love, even in its brokenness, could still be worth fighting for.

Nine

The Revealing of the Song

The air was thick with tension, vibrating with an energy that neither Selisyn nor Thalior could fully comprehend. They stood at the threshold of the ancient library of Maelithra Daryon, the scholar who had warned them of the price of their eternal bond. The room was vast, its stone walls covered in moss, and shelves that seemed to stretch into infinity. The dim light from the flickering torches cast long shadows across the floor, distorting the shapes of the texts that lined the shelves—some of them older than time itself.

Selisyn could feel the weight of the place, the burden of the secrets hidden in its depths. And yet, the pull of the song—the hollow, haunting melody that had threaded its way through every moment of their lives—was stronger. It lingered in the background of her thoughts, always present, a reminder of the curse they were bound to. She could hear it now, like a whisper on the wind, threading through the air like a ribbon of pain and longing.

"What are we going to find here, Thalior?" she asked, her voice barely more than a breath. Her fingers clutched the edge of a weathered table, trying to ground herself in the moment. The uncertainty gnawed at her, a growing feeling that they were about to discover something that would change everything—something they might not be able to undo.

Thalior's gaze swept over the room, his expression tight, his jaw clenched as if he, too, could sense the danger of what lay ahead. "The truth," he said, his voice grim. "We've come too far to turn back now. It's time we learn exactly what we're dealing with."

He stepped forward, his hand brushing a stack of ancient scrolls as if searching for something, some key that would unlock the mystery of their past, of the song. It had been their constant companion, the haunting melody woven into their lives, driving them into each other's arms only to pull them apart again. It had defined their love, twisted it, and now it threatened to tear them apart once more.

Selisyn could feel her heart race in her chest. "But what if the truth is worse than we imagine?"

Thalior turned to face her, his expression softening. His eyes, usually so full of strength and resolve, now held a flicker of vulnerability. "What if it's the only way out? We have to know, Selisyn. We have to break this cycle. For both of us."

She nodded, her throat tight. There was no choice. They had come too far to stop now. But deep inside, a whisper of doubt curled in her heart. Could they survive the truth?

The sound of footsteps broke the silence, echoing through the vast, cavernous space. A figure appeared from the

The Revealing of the Song

shadows—a tall, cloaked figure, their face hidden in the folds of the hood. The air seemed to shift when the figure stepped into the light, the temperature dropping, the shadows darkening.

"You seek the truth," the figure said, their voice a strange, melodic hum that resonated in Selisyn's bones. "But the truth is not easily uncovered, nor is it easily borne."

"Who are you?" Selisyn demanded, stepping forward, her hand instinctively moving to her side, as if preparing for a fight. "What do you know of the song?"

The figure's hooded head tilted slightly, as though amused by her response. "I am Fionan Valtor," the figure replied, their voice now clearer, yet still carrying an otherworldly quality. "And I know much of the song. For it is tied to the very fabric of this realm. It was never meant to be broken."

"Then why are we here?" Thalior asked, his tone demanding. "What is this song? And why does it haunt us?"

Fionan stepped forward, revealing a face that seemed ageless, neither young nor old, but with eyes that shimmered like the stars in a night sky. There was wisdom in those eyes, but also a deep, unsettling knowledge—knowledge of things best left forgotten.

"The song," Fionan began, "is not merely a melody. It is a force. A living, breathing entity that exists beyond the realms of time and space. It is The Singularity."

The name struck like a bolt of lightning, and Selisyn's breath caught in her throat. The Singularity. She had heard whispers of it in the dreams that had plagued her—vague images, fleeting glimpses of something terrible, something vast. But she had never imagined it was real.

Fionan's eyes locked with hers, and Selisyn felt the weight of their gaze, as if the very essence of the being standing before her was reaching into her soul. "The Singularity is not just a force that binds time and love," Fionan continued. "It is a sentient being, one that feeds on the power of those bound by love and loss. It thrives on your pain, on the cycles of longing and sorrow that have shaped your existence."

Thalior stepped forward, his voice sharp with disbelief. "Are you saying that the song—this… thing—is controlling us? That it created us?"

Fionan nodded. "Yes. The Singularity is the architect of your bond. It has woven you together, not as lovers, but as prisoners. You are bound to it, and it to you, for all eternity. It feeds off your emotions, your pain, your love, and your loss. The cycles you've lived, the endless replays of love and death, have been orchestrated by it."

Selisyn stumbled back, her hand going to her chest as though the words themselves had struck her. "No… no, it can't be. We've chosen each other, we've fought for this love…"

"Fighting does not make it real," Fionan interrupted, his voice gentle but firm. "You were not meant to be together, not like this. The Singularity chose you, bound you together to feed off your souls, to keep you in this endless cycle."

Thalior's face twisted in anger, his fists clenching at his sides. "So, we were never free? We were never really in control of our love? We've been nothing but pawns in this game?"

Fionan's eyes softened with a sorrowful understanding. "You are not pawns, Thalior. But you are bound. Your love, your pain, your endless struggle—it has all been part of a greater design. A design forged by the realm's dark ruler, who sought to bind you, to use your souls as instruments in their twisted creation."

Selisyn felt her legs go weak, and she leaned against a nearby column to steady herself. This was too much. Too much to bear. But still, a part of her had known. Hadn't she always felt that something had been wrong? That something about their bond had been too... perfect? Too painful?

"What can we do?" she whispered, her voice barely audible. "How can we break free?"

Fionan's gaze shifted to the shadows that seemed to close in around them, a reflection of the dark power that lingered in the air. "There is one way," Fionan said. "But it will not be easy. You are the creators of this song, Selisyn and Thalior. In a past life, you wove the melody together, binding your souls to the very fabric of the song. Only by severing your connection to it—by breaking the bond between you—can you free yourselves."

Selisyn's heart skipped a beat. "You want us to give up our love?" Her voice cracked. "After everything we've been through?"

Fionan nodded solemnly. "Love, as you know it, must be sacrificed. Only then can you escape the song. Only then can you sever the chains that bind you."

For a moment, there was silence. The weight of the decision, the cost of it, hung between them like an unbearable burden. The love they had fought for, the bond they had built—it would all be gone.

But then, amidst the overwhelming tide of emotions, Selisyn understood. The truth was clear, even though it was painful. The cycle had to end. No matter the cost.

She turned to Thalior, her gaze meeting his for the first time since they had entered this place. He looked as lost as she felt, but there was a spark in his eyes, a flicker of understanding.

"This is it," she whispered. "We have to choose."

The Hollow Song of Eternity

Thalior reached out to her, his hand trembling as it brushed against hers. "Together, Selisyn. Always. No matter what."

The tension in the air grew thicker, and the song, that haunting melody that had always been a part of them, seemed to pulse louder, more insistent. But this time, Selisyn could feel something else beneath the surface—something dark, something powerful. The Singularity was watching them. Waiting for them to make their choice.

And in that moment, they both knew that the path ahead would not be easy. There would be no easy answers, no safe way out. But they had come this far, and now, they had to face the truth—the full truth—of what their love had become.

With a deep breath, Selisyn spoke again. "We will break the song. We will free ourselves."

Thalior nodded, his grip tightening on her hand.

The battle had just begun.

The silence between them was heavy, a crushing weight that settled deep within Selisyn's chest. The decision had been made, but its consequences loomed like an impossible chasm. She glanced at Thalior, his face a mirror of her own inner turmoil. His eyes were shadowed, filled with a mixture of dread and resolve, as if he too could feel the enormity of what they had just agreed to.

Yet beneath that veil of uncertainty, there was something else—something pure, something undeniable. Their hands still clasped together, a silent promise that they were no longer just two souls bound by an ancient force. They were a united front, a single, resolute entity that would stand against the storm. But even that certainty began to crack under the weight of the truth that had been revealed.

Fionan's voice shattered the quiet.

"Before you proceed," Fionan said, stepping back into the shadows, his form becoming an indistinct silhouette. "You must understand that this is not merely a severing of love. You must destroy it—obliterate the bond entirely. Once you sever it, there will be no turning back. The song will be erased, but so too will your connection to one another."

The words sank deep into Selisyn's soul, pulling at the very core of her being. She had thought she was ready, but the thought of losing Thalior—of having no thread left to bind her to him—made her stomach turn. Could she survive without him? She had been haunted by the song for so long, drawn into its endless cycle, that the idea of freedom now felt foreign. The music had been their constant, the ever-present rhythm that shaped the very core of their love and pain. To break it, to destroy the melody… it was like erasing them.

"But—" Thalior's voice broke through her reverie, and she turned toward him, her heart twisting at the vulnerability in his eyes. "What will become of us then? If we sever the song… what happens to our souls? To who we are?"

Fionan didn't answer right away. Instead, there was a long pause, as though the ancient being was weighing the gravity of their question. Finally, the figure spoke, the words slow and deliberate, each one seeming to carry the weight of ages.

"You will be free," Fionan replied. "But you will be strangers to one another. Your love, the force that binds you now, will be gone. You will no longer remember the moments that shaped you, the laughter and tears you shared. The memories will fade, erased as if they never existed."

The horror of it set in slowly, creeping like an insidious poison. The depth of their connection, the tender memories of stolen moments, the promises they had made to each other—they would all vanish. She would lose the very essence of who she had become, the part of herself that was intertwined with Thalior.

Selisyn's hand trembled in his, but she didn't pull away. Instead, she squeezed his fingers tighter, grounding herself in the present moment, in the touch of the man who had fought beside her through endless trials, even when they had not known the full truth. The man whose soul seemed to shine brighter with each passing day, whose love, despite the pain and uncertainty, had been the one constant in her existence.

But now, the very thing that had defined them—love—was the thing they had to destroy.

Thalior's voice was hoarse when he spoke again. "And if we choose not to sever it? What will happen to us?"

Fionan's expression shifted, the shadows beneath his hood deepening. "The Singularity will tighten its hold. The song will grow stronger, more insistent. It will consume you, piece by piece. And in the end, you will be nothing but puppets in its endless dance. Your love will become your prison. The cycles will never end. You will repeat this eternal loop until you can no longer tell who you are—until your very souls are consumed by the melody."

The words echoed in Selisyn's mind, and she closed her eyes for a moment, feeling the weight of their consequences. Was there any choice? Could they live forever bound by the song, doomed to repeat their pain, their love, and their loss in an endless, torturous cycle?

"I don't want that," Thalior murmured, his voice breaking through her thoughts. "I don't want to be trapped forever, Selisyn. I don't want you to be trapped."

Her heart ached at the desperation in his voice, and for a brief moment, she could almost hear the echoes of that song—the hollow tune that had haunted them for so long. It felt so familiar, so painful, and yet it was not the worst thing they had faced. What was worse was the uncertainty now, the sheer unknown of what came next. What was left after the song?

She turned to face him fully, her breath coming in shallow gasps, her heart pounding. "But will we lose each other? Will I lose you?"

The question hung in the air, heavy with the weight of everything they had been through. Thalior's eyes softened, and he reached up, gently cupping her face in his hands. His touch was warm, grounding, like the very thing that made her real, made her whole.

"If it means being free, if it means ending this pain, I'll do whatever it takes, Selisyn," he whispered. "Even if it means I have to lose you. But I won't lose you willingly, not without a fight. If there's any chance of us staying together, I'll find it."

Her chest tightened, and for a moment, she could hardly breathe. There was no easy way out. No perfect solution. The choice between freedom and love had never been so impossible to make.

Fionan, watching them, seemed to sense the turmoil in their hearts, for he spoke again, this time more softly.

"The choice is yours, Selisyn and Thalior. But remember this: the cost of freedom is not a simple one. If you sever your bond, you will be free. But you will also be cast into the unknown. You may never see each other again, and even if you do, you will not recognize each other. Your connection will be severed completely, as if it had never existed."

Selisyn's thoughts raced, the weight of the decision pressing on her chest. The freedom they had longed for was within reach, but it came at a price higher than anything they had ever imagined. They could escape the cycle. They could be free. But it meant letting go of everything they had known, everything they had fought for. Could they do that?

"Please," she whispered, her voice cracking. "Tell me there's another way. Tell me there's a way to keep what we have."

Fionan's eyes softened, and for a moment, he almost looked... sympathetic. "There is no other way, Selisyn. Not unless you wish to continue in the song, to continue your endless cycle. The Singularity will not allow you to escape unless you sever the bond completely."

Thalior took a deep breath and exhaled slowly, his hand slipping from hers, leaving a cold void in its place. It was the first time in all their time together that they had felt truly apart. The song hummed softly in the background, pulling at them like invisible threads, but now the melody felt distant, muted. As if it, too, was waiting for them to make their choice.

Selisyn closed her eyes, trying to steady her thoughts, her heart. She felt as if the weight of the world rested on her shoulders. What would they do? What would she do? And what would it cost them both?

"I... I can't lose you," she whispered, her voice thick with emotion. "But I can't live like this anymore either."

Thalior's hand brushed against hers once more, his touch a lifeline in the midst of the storm that raged between them. His voice was steady, though his words held the tremor of uncertainty.

"We will make it through this, Selisyn," he said. "We will find a way, together. No matter what."

Her chest tightened, and she felt the weight of everything.

The Revealing of the Song

The decision was coming. The moment was close.

And then, the song began to play again.

This time, it wasn't a gentle whisper. It was loud, insistent. A pulse, deep and powerful, reverberating in the very air around them. A reminder of everything they had lost and everything they stood to gain. It seemed to echo in their very bones.

And they both knew, without a doubt, that the time for choosing was at hand. The song had returned, and so had the cost.

Ten

The Path of Sacrifice

The sky above them was a roiling mass of darkness, the very air thick with tension. It felt as if time itself had slowed, stretching into infinity as Selisyn and Thalior stood at the edge of the Abyss of Time. The ground beneath their feet was a jagged expanse of blackened stone, twisted in impossible shapes, as though reality itself had warped and fractured at the very threshold of this forsaken place. The Abyss stretched before them like a gaping maw, a chasm of unimaginable depth, its very presence pulling at the edges of their minds. The air was heavy with an unnatural stillness, the faintest hum of power vibrating through the earth like the pulse of a heart too large to fathom.

Selisyn could feel it in her bones—the weight of the decision they had made. The path ahead was a one-way journey, and the cost was unimaginable. The very fabric of their existence was now entwined with the choice they would soon make. Her chest tightened, her heart struggling against the uncertainty that had settled within her.

"I don't know if I can do this," she whispered, her voice barely audible, lost beneath the oppressive silence that surrounded them.

Thalior's presence beside her was a constant, a reminder of everything they had fought for. But even his steady strength couldn't quell the storm within her. He was the one constant in her life—her love, her anchor. How could they tear themselves apart for freedom? How could they sacrifice everything they had, everything they had become, just to escape a fate that had already shaped them for eternity?

"You don't have to do this alone," Thalior said, his voice low and soothing, though she could hear the uncertainty there, too. He didn't know the answer either. "Whatever it is we must do, we do it together."

Her gaze met his, and for a moment, she allowed herself to look beyond the fear, to see the man who had stood beside her through every battle, every heartache. He had shared in her pain, in her triumphs, and in their darkest hours. And now, as they stood on the precipice of the end, she could not imagine facing it without him.

But there was no avoiding it. No other way.

"We're already bound by the song," she said, her voice trembling slightly. "If we don't do this, we will be lost forever, trapped in a loop we can't escape. But if we sacrifice…"

Thalior reached for her hand, squeezing it with a strength that sent a surge of warmth through her. "We're already lost, Selisyn. The choice is not between being lost or found. It's between fighting for each other… and fighting for ourselves."

She nodded, unable to speak as a lump formed in her throat.

It was a cold, jagged thing, lodged deep in her chest. How could they give up what they had fought so hard to build? Was love so fragile that it could be undone with a single sacrifice?

"I think I'm ready," Thalior continued, his gaze unwavering as he looked into her eyes. "But are you?"

The question lingered between them, heavy and suffocating. They both knew the answer. They had no choice. But even as she nodded, her heart threatened to tear itself apart. They had come this far, and yet the abyss before them seemed to swallow every shred of hope they had left.

Together, they moved forward, their footsteps echoing in the vast emptiness of the Abyss. As they ventured deeper into the chasm, the air grew colder, and a sense of wrongness gnawed at the edges of their consciousness. The song—the melody that had tied them together for centuries—hung in the air, a faint hum beneath the silence, as though it was watching them, waiting for them to make their move.

And then, as they reached the center of the Abyss, the ground before them split open, and from the depths emerged a figure.

The man was tall, his presence imposing, his body cloaked in the dark, tattered robes of a forgotten age. His face was hidden beneath a hood, but Selisyn could feel his gaze cutting through her, piercing her very soul. There was something ancient about him, something that spoke of time itself—like he had been there before the world began and would remain after it had all crumbled to dust.

"You are brave," the figure said, his voice like the grinding of stones, deep and resonant. "But bravery alone will not see you through the trials of the Abyss."

Torianth Vallis, the ancient guardian, stepped forward, his dark robes swirling around him like a storm. The air seemed to bend around him, as if the very fabric of reality was warping in his presence.

"You seek to destroy The Singularity," he continued, his voice carrying the weight of ages. "You seek to break the song and free yourselves from its grasp. But do you understand the cost of what you ask?"

Selisyn swallowed hard, her throat dry. The weight of his words settled heavily on her shoulders. She wanted to scream, to demand that he tell them what they had to do to end this madness. But she knew. Deep down, she knew. The cost would be more than just a simple choice.

"Tell us what we must do," Thalior said, his voice steady but strained, as though he too understood the depths of what was being asked of them.

Torianth's eyes gleamed beneath the hood, and for the first time, Selisyn saw a glimmer of pity in them.

"The Singularity is bound to time itself," the guardian explained. "It is the very force that has shaped your lives, your love, and your suffering. To sever it is to sever the very core of what makes you... you. The bond that connects you to the song is what gives your love its strength, its power. If you destroy it, you will lose everything. Your memories, your emotions, your very souls. The love that binds you will be erased."

"Erased?" Selisyn echoed, her voice a whisper of disbelief. "What do you mean, erased? You're saying... we'll never remember?"

"Yes," Torianth answered, his voice cold and final. "You will forget each other. The song will be no more. But so too will your love. It will be as if it never existed."

A chill ran down Selisyn's spine, and her heart clenched painfully in her chest. Thalior's hand tightened around hers, his grip a silent promise that they would face this together. But the truth of the guardian's words was undeniable. If they went through with this, they would be severed from everything they had known. Every touch, every kiss, every whispered word of love—gone. Lost to time. Would they even be able to recognize each other without the memories of what they had shared?

"You are asking us to choose between love and freedom," Selisyn said, her voice trembling. "To sever the bond that has defined us... or to remain imprisoned by it forever."

Torianth nodded slowly. "That is the choice you face. But remember, the path of sacrifice is not one to take lightly. Once the song is broken, it will never return. You will not be the same. And neither will the world."

She looked at Thalior, searching his eyes for some sign, some indication of what he was thinking. His gaze met hers, steady and unwavering, though she could see the storm raging behind them. He was just as torn as she was. But in that moment, she knew that he would sacrifice anything—everything—to break free of the chains that bound them. Even if it meant losing her.

"Tell us what we need to do," Thalior said quietly, his voice resolute.

Torianth stepped forward, raising his hand as a glowing sigil appeared beneath them, casting an eerie light across the Abyss. "To break the bond, one of you must be willing to give up your life. A life for a life. It is the only way."

Selisyn's breath caught in her throat. The weight of the decision settled upon her like a crushing force. She knew what he was asking. One of them had to die. One of them had to be willing to make the ultimate sacrifice for the other.

"No..." she whispered, her voice barely audible.

But Thalior's voice cut through her thoughts, firm and

unwavering.

"I will do it," he said.

Selisyn's heart stopped. She looked at him, disbelief washing over her. "No," she whispered again, this time more urgently. "Thalior, no. I can't let you—"

"You have to," he interrupted softly. "You've already sacrificed so much. Let me do this for you. Let me set you free."

The words hung in the air between them, as heavy as the chasm below. This was it. The choice had been made. And now, there was no turning back.

Torianth's gaze shifted to the sigil, and the light beneath them grew brighter, hotter, as if the Abyss itself was preparing to swallow them whole.

"Once the sacrifice is made," Torianth said, his voice grave, "the song will be destroyed. And the bond you share will be severed. But remember, the cost is eternal. Once you take this step, there is no coming back."

Selisyn's world tilted, the ground beneath her feet shifting as she looked at Thalior. He was resolute, but she could see the pain in his eyes. She could feel the depth of his love for her. And in that moment, she understood. There was no choice to be made.

He had already made it for both of them.

The sigil beneath their feet pulsed with an eerie light, casting shadows that seemed to dance and writhe like living things. It beckoned them forward, a dark, irresistible call that thrummed through the very air they breathed. Selisyn stood frozen, her gaze locked on the glowing pattern, and for the briefest moment, she imagined that the world had paused—time itself suspended in the weight of the choice that hung between them.

The Hollow Song of Eternity

Thalior's words echoed in her mind, though they sounded distant and hollow. *Let me set you free.* He had already made his decision. There was no more time for questioning, no more room for hesitation. The path was clear now. One would live. One would die. And they would be torn apart forever.

"I don't want this," Selisyn whispered, the words slipping from her lips before she could stop them. Her hand tightened on Thalior's, desperately grasping at the only piece of him that was still real. "I can't let you do this. You—"

"Selisyn," Thalior said softly, his voice breaking through her panic. He cupped her face, his thumb gently brushing the tear that had slipped down her cheek. His touch was a lifeline, pulling her back from the brink of despair. "I don't want this either. But I want you to be free more than anything. I would die a thousand times if it meant you could live without the shadow of the song over you."

His words were as much a promise as a confession, and they struck deep within her chest. The bond that had tied them together for so long now felt like a trap, a chain wrapped around both their hearts, its weight unbearable. She had always believed that love was supposed to be freeing, that it would elevate them both. But now, as they stood in this forsaken place, the truth was clear: love, at least as they had known it, was a prison. The only way to break free was to sever the very thing that had bound them.

"I can't forget you, Thalior. I can't imagine a world without you in it," Selisyn murmured, her voice breaking, tears now flowing freely down her face. She shook her head as if trying to deny the truth that was being forced upon them. "You're everything. How can I lose you?"

Thalior's hands moved to her shoulders, his grip firm and

reassuring despite the storm raging within him. "Selisyn, listen to me. This isn't about forgetting. This isn't about losing you. It's about breaking the chains that have kept us both trapped. We've been bound by the song for too long. The past, our love, the pain... all of it is a cycle we can't escape unless we do this. You know this."

She closed her eyes, squeezing the tears from her lashes. She could feel his words taking root inside her heart, gnawing at her, digging deep into the soil of her soul. She could feel it, too—the weight of their shared suffering, the centuries of love and loss that had repeated over and over like a broken record. The song had never given them peace; it had only enslaved them in its endless loop.

But to let go of him now? To let him make the sacrifice? It was unthinkable.

"I love you," she whispered, her voice barely audible. She said the words as if they were a lifeline, something to tether her to him just a little longer. "I love you, Thalior. But I can't let you die for me."

He didn't answer immediately. Instead, his gaze searched hers, as if trying to see beyond her fear and uncertainty, into the very core of her being. Then, his expression softened, and he kissed her gently, his lips warm and familiar against her skin, bringing with it a bittersweet comfort.

"I love you, too," he murmured, his voice barely audible against her lips. "But this is the only way."

The sound of his words reverberated in her chest, echoing like the song that had held them captive for so long. Her mind swirled with the thoughts of all they had endured—of all they had lost and gained in this strange, twisted existence they called love. Was it possible for love to survive without the promise of forever? Could they truly live free of the chains that had bound them, even if it meant breaking apart to do so?

The choice was unbearable. The decision felt too heavy, too final. Selisyn pulled away from Thalior's embrace, her heart racing as the weight of the choice pressed against her like a thousand storms. The Abyss of Time, the sigil beneath them, and Torianth's chilling words all loomed in the background, making her feel small, insignificant, and powerless in the face of it all.

But there was no more time. There was no more room to delay. She had to act.

"How can I choose?" she asked, her voice cracking. "How do I know if this is the right thing to do? If we destroy the song, if we break the bond, will we ever even find our way back to each other? Will we remember what we had, what we meant to each other? Or will we be nothing more than two strangers who once shared a fleeting connection?"

Torianth's voice cut through the air, cold and final. "You will remember nothing. Not your love. Not the moments you shared. Not even the pain. Once the bond is broken, the past will be erased, and only what you have left—your souls, untainted by the song—will remain."

The truth of his words was a knife through her heart. To lose Thalior was to lose herself, to lose everything she had ever known. But to remain bound by the song was to continue in torment forever, never truly free. There was no easy way out. No simple solution.

"I don't want to forget you," she whispered, her voice choked with emotion. "I can't."

Thalior stepped closer to her, his hand brushing her cheek in a tender, final gesture. "You won't forget. You will be free,

Selisyn. And if we are meant to find each other again, we will. But this… this is the only way. If we don't make this choice, we will be trapped in this cycle forever."

She looked into his eyes, and for the first time in what felt like an eternity, she saw the truth there. The love that had once been a bond now felt like a prison, the walls closing in on them. And no matter how much she wanted to deny it, to hold onto him and their love forever, she knew deep within her heart that he was right.

It had to end. Their love, their pain, their suffering—it all had to end, so they could be free.

Selisyn closed her eyes, her breath coming in shallow gasps as the tears continued to fall. Her chest ached with the enormity of what she was about to lose. And yet, there was a strange peace in her heart, a quiet understanding that this was the only way forward. This was the only way to give both of them the chance at a life beyond the song, beyond the endless loop of love and loss.

"Do it," she whispered, the words a tremor of finality. "I'll let you go, Thalior. I'll let you go so that we can be free."

His gaze never wavered as he nodded, his lips trembling as he fought to hold back his own tears. "Thank you," he said softly. "I love you."

And then, as if the words themselves had summoned it, the sigil beneath their feet flared to life, its light growing blindingly bright. The ground beneath them cracked open, and Selisyn felt herself being pulled away from Thalior, as if the very fabric of reality was tearing. The Abyss beneath them swirled with an overwhelming force, its depths a black pit of endless nothingness.

In that instant, as she felt herself being torn away from

everything she had ever known, Selisyn realized the truth: love, no matter how pure, no matter how strong, could not save them from the darkness. Only sacrifice could free them.

And as the world around her shattered, she whispered one last word, her voice barely a breath against the growing storm.

"Goodbye."

Eleven

The Heart of the Storm

The sky above them split open with a violent crack, as though the heavens themselves had been torn in two. The wind howled, a piercing wail that seemed to come from everywhere and nowhere at once. The very air around them thickened, a tangible force pressing against their chests, suffocating them. Selisyn could feel the storm clawing at her skin, the power of the song manifesting in the world around them, warping reality and time itself.

The ground beneath her feet trembled, and the sky above them churned like a roiling sea, dark clouds swirling with unnatural speed. Lightning streaked across the sky in jagged arcs, illuminating the scene with flashes of raw, blinding light. Thunder followed in its wake, the sound so deep and resonant that it felt as though the entire world was shaking under the weight of it.

Beside her, Thalior stumbled, his expression grim as he

looked up into the chaos above them. His hand shot out to grip her wrist, pulling her closer, as though trying to shield her from the storm. But there was no escape from this. No shelter. The storm was not just a force of nature; it was a manifestation of the very essence that had bound them, the song that had kept them chained in this endless cycle of love and loss.

"Selisyn," Thalior shouted, his voice barely audible over the roar of the wind. "We have to move!"

She nodded, but her heart was heavy with dread. The storm was more than just a physical threat. She could feel it, deep in her bones—the power of the song, pulling at them, threatening to tear them apart. The song had always been a force of control, and now, in the heart of this storm, it seemed to have reached its peak. Time itself was unraveling. Reality was bending.

Suddenly, the world around them seemed to twist, the ground beneath their feet warping like liquid. Selisyn gasped as the landscape shifted and buckled, and the next moment, the world seemed to fall away entirely. She was no longer standing on solid ground. She was falling, plunging into the dark void of the storm, her body weightless, as though she were suspended between worlds.

A scream tore from her throat as she reached out, desperate to find something—anything—to hold onto. Her fingers brushed against nothingness, and for a moment, she thought she might be swallowed whole by the storm, lost forever in its fury.

But then, in the blink of an eye, everything changed. The sensation of falling stopped. She found herself standing in a different place entirely—one that felt both familiar and utterly foreign at the same time. The air was thick with an oppressive silence, and the landscape stretched out before her in dark, muted tones. It was a vision—a memory, she realized, a twisted reflection of the past that had never truly been laid to rest.

She turned, her heart thundering in her chest, and saw him. Thalior.

But it was not the Thalior she knew. This was another version of him, a version that belonged to another life, another time. He stood in front of her, his eyes filled with an agony she could feel in her own chest. His expression was torn, conflicted, as though he were struggling with some unspeakable choice.

The world around them shimmered, as though reality itself was buckling under the weight of their emotions. And then, she saw it—the moment. The betrayal. The moment that had shattered everything in their past life.

It was as if the very air around them had thickened with a terrible anticipation. The Queen's throne room stretched out before her, opulent and cold. The stone walls seemed to close in on them, the shadows long and oppressive. The grandeur of the room was lost in the tension, the bitter weight of words unspoken and decisions made.

Thalior stood before her, his eyes dark and distant, his posture rigid with something that wasn't just anger but regret. She felt it in the very core of her being—the coldness, the distance. He was no longer the man who had held her, who had loved her. He was something else entirely.

"Selisyn..." he murmured, his voice hollow, like a ghost calling from the depths of time. His eyes searched her face, and for a moment, she saw the flicker of love, but it was quickly smothered by something darker, something that held him back. "I—I couldn't do it. I couldn't risk it."

The words landed like a blow to her chest. She could feel the betrayal rising in her throat, choking her.

"You couldn't risk it?" she whispered, her voice shaking. "What is this, Thalior? What have you done? We were meant to be together. I—"

But her words were cut off as a shadow passed between them, like a dark cloud moving through the light. It was as though the room itself was rejecting their love, twisting it into something unrecognizable.

Thalior's face twisted in pain as he turned away, his back to her. "I couldn't let the kingdom fall, Selisyn. You were everything to me, but you were also the queen. I couldn't let you risk everything for me."

Her chest tightened, and the world around her blurred, shifting like a mirror that couldn't hold its shape. The reality of their past life—the pain, the heartbreak, the choices they had made—saturated the air, thick and heavy. She wanted to scream, to stop him, to make him see reason. But she could do nothing. She was bound, a mere observer to their past mistakes.

In that moment, she felt herself pulled away again, yanked out of the vision. The world around her shifted violently, and she found herself back in the storm, the howling wind crashing against her like a physical force. Her heart hammered in her chest as she gasped for breath, the vision still burning in her mind.

But it wasn't over. Not by a long shot.

Her gaze snapped to Thalior. He was kneeling on the ground, his hands clutching his head as though he were in agony. His body trembled, and his eyes were wide with terror.

"No," he breathed, his voice choked with fear. "No, not again. Not like this."

Selisyn staggered toward him, reaching out for him, but as

The Heart of the Storm

her hands neared, the storm intensified. The wind howled, whipping around her, threatening to tear her apart. She could barely hear him over the deafening roar of the storm, but she saw it in his eyes—he was reliving it again, the betrayal, the moment when everything had shattered between them.

"Thalior!" Selisyn shouted, her voice barely carrying over the storm. She threw herself at him, her hands grasping his shoulders, pulling him back toward her. But the vision of their past life persisted, playing out again and again like a broken record.

And then, a new vision—one that made Selisyn's blood run cold—unfolded before her.

She saw herself, not in the past, but in the future. A future where Thalior was gone. She saw herself standing alone, empty, her heart hollow. The love they had once shared was nothing but a faint memory, a whisper in the dark. She watched herself wither away in the silence, the space between them growing wider and colder with each passing day.

Her breath hitched in her throat as the vision shifted again, and she saw Thalior—this time, not in the past or the future, but in the present—his eyes dark, empty, as though he had forgotten her entirely. The love they had shared was gone, erased from his memory, and he was nothing more than a stranger.

"No!" she cried, stumbling backward, her heart shattering. "No, this can't be—"

But as the storm raged around her, the truth settled in her chest like a heavy stone. The question she had feared, the question she had never wanted to ask—*did they truly deserve each other?*

The storm raged on, time fracturing, reality warping. The

heart of the storm was not just the fury of the elements, but the fear that had been woven into the very fabric of their bond. The fear that no matter how much they loved each other, the darkness of their past—of their mistakes—would always tear them apart.

And as the storm raged on, Selisyn knew one thing with a certainty she could not escape: they were facing the heart of the storm—not the tempest of the elements, but the tempest of their own hearts, their own fears.

And the question remained.

Would they ever truly be free?

The storm's grip tightened, like the jaws of an unseen beast. Selisyn staggered, her legs unsteady as the violent winds seemed to push her in every direction. She fought against them, but her movements were slow, deliberate, as though the very air was conspiring to hold her in place, forcing her to confront the raw truth of their bond.

She turned back toward Thalior, her heart hammering in her chest, and the sight of him struck her like a blow. He was kneeling, clutching his head, his body rigid with tension. The vision of his betrayal still lingered in the space between them, as real and as painful as if it had just happened. The storm seemed to reflect the chaos within him, the agony of reliving his own mistakes, his guilt tearing at him, just as it was tearing at her.

"Thalior!" she cried again, her voice desperate, carried away by the wind, but she could see the torment in his eyes. The light in them was dim, as though the weight of their past was crushing the soul she knew, and with it, the love they had fought so hard to find again.

"No, no, not again," Thalior gasped, his voice cracking with the weight of his memories. "I can't... I can't live through this again. I—"

But the words trailed off as the storm roared louder, the dark clouds swirling above them, swirling around him, their tendrils wrapping around him like the hands of an invisible enemy. Selisyn's heart wrenched, and she tried to reach for him, but the moment her fingers brushed his shoulder, everything shifted again.

In the blink of an eye, Selisyn found herself back within the vision—the same dark room, the throne room that had witnessed the birth of their undoing. She was standing across from Thalior, and this time, the sense of betrayal hit her like a physical blow, drowning her in the weight of the past.

His face was a mask of pain, his jaw clenched, and his eyes darted between the ground and her face, as if he couldn't bear to meet her gaze. His form trembled with the burden of his decision, but there was no escaping it. The past was unshakable.

"You always loved the kingdom more than me," Selisyn whispered, the words carrying a quiet venom. The weight of them was more than she could bear.

"I loved you," Thalior responded, but his voice cracked, betraying him. "But I couldn't bear to see you sacrifice everything for us. I thought I was protecting you. Protecting us."

The words were poison to her, twisting in her chest. "Protecting me?" she spat. "By betraying me? By betraying our love?"

She could feel the darkness creeping into her soul, creeping into the very essence of their love. The shadows that had been present since the moment they had first met, the weight of the curse, were now rising, pushing them further apart with every passing second. The room was suffocating, heavy with the ghost of their history. Time bent and shifted, pulling them back into the cruel cycle of their bond.

But then, the room darkened further, and the shadow that had been lurking in the corners of their love emerged fully. It was not just the pain of betrayal that surrounded them but a deeper, more insidious force. The presence of The Singularity was overwhelming, like a dark, pulsing energy, wrapping around them like chains.

The storm above them mirrored the terror of that moment, as if the very sky was mourning their lost love, mocking them for ever believing they could escape the pull of the song.

Thalior's eyes widened in realization, and he looked at Selisyn, his gaze filled with an unspoken plea. "Selisyn, please," he whispered, "we have to break this cycle. We can't let it consume us again. This is what The Singularity wants—this is its design. It wants us to break each other, to tear us apart so it can feed on our pain."

But before Selisyn could respond, the darkness around them deepened, and the storm's winds surged with an otherworldly force, slamming into them both. The world began to fracture, as though time itself were splintering like shattered glass.

A powerful force pulled Selisyn away from Thalior, ripping her from his side. She was hurled into another vision, one even darker and more suffocating than the last. This time, she found herself in a desolate landscape, void of color and life. The sky was a sickly shade of gray, and the earth beneath her feet cracked and crumbled. There was no wind here, no sound—just a suffocating silence that pressed in from all sides.

In the distance, she saw a figure. A lone silhouette standing at the edge of the horizon, its features obscured by the mists that clung to the ground. But there was something familiar about the shape. Something hauntingly familiar.

As she took a step forward, she saw it—the figure was her, or at least someone who looked like her. But this version of herself was cold, distant, her eyes lifeless, her expression hardened and weary. This was not the woman she had been, but the woman she could become.

It was a future she didn't want to face. A future where she stood alone, separated from Thalior, consumed by her fears, by the storm that had torn them apart.

"No," Selisyn breathed, stepping back. "This isn't real. This can't be real."

But the vision held firm. The image of herself continued to advance, until the two versions of her were face-to-face. She looked into her own eyes and saw the emptiness that would swallow her if she gave in.

"You're too weak, Selisyn," the other her said, her voice cold and emotionless. "You always have been. That's why you'll never have him. You'll never be worthy of his love."

The words burned into Selisyn's chest like a poison, and the shadows that had been gathering in the distance began to move closer, crawling like serpents toward her. The storm intensified once more, the winds howling with fury.

"No!" Selisyn shouted, slamming her palms to her ears, trying to block out the words, but they echoed in her mind, relentless and suffocating. "I am not weak. I am not!"

But the shadows only grew, pressing in on her. She stumbled backward, her breath coming in ragged gasps. She could feel the storm closing in on her, the pressure on her chest like the weight of the world.

Somewhere, deep in the distance, she heard Thalior's voice, calling her name, but it was distorted, muffled, like it was being swallowed by the storm. She tried to reach for him, to call back to him, but the vision held her fast. The world was crumbling around her, and she was falling into the abyss, unable to stop it.

She could feel herself slipping away, the edges of her reality blurring. Her heart ached with the loss of the love she had once held so fiercely. She wanted to fight, wanted to push back against the storm, against the darkness that sought to swallow her whole.

But there was only one thing she knew for certain—*the song* had always been their greatest enemy. And now, it had come to claim them.

But Thalior's voice reached her again, louder this time. His words were a lifeline in the overwhelming storm.

"Selisyn!" he cried, his voice cutting through the noise of the tempest. "You are not weak! You never were. Come back to me! We will face this together!"

His words were like a beacon of light in the storm, and for a moment, everything stilled. The shadows hesitated, the storm's roar softened, and in that stillness, Selisyn took a step forward. She reached out with trembling hands, and with every ounce of strength she had left, she broke through the vision.

Thalior's presence, his touch, grounded her. He was there, standing before her in the storm, his eyes filled with determination. The winds howled, but now they seemed to pale in comparison to the strength of their bond.

"We are not lost," Selisyn whispered, her voice steady. "We will break this. Together."

The Heart of the Storm

And with that, they stood together, facing the storm, knowing that the darkest trials were yet to come. But this time, they would not face them alone.

Twelve

The Betrayal Revisited

The storm above them had intensified, its ferocity eclipsing anything they had experienced before. The winds howled like the cries of tormented souls, and the air crackled with an energy that seemed to pulse with dark intention. The sky swirled with shades of crimson and violet, a reflection of the violent emotions that gripped Selisyn and Thalior in its depths. Their journey had led them to this moment, but neither of them was prepared for what the storm would reveal.

Selisyn stood with her back pressed against the jagged, black rocks of the Abyss, her breath ragged as she tried to steady herself against the force of the wind. The song, that cursed melody that had always haunted their souls, throbbed in the air, an eerie and unrelenting hum that vibrated through the very fabric of reality. The storm was not just a manifestation of nature, but of the power that bound them. It had become something living, something aware of their every doubt, every fear, every fracture in their connection.

She turned her gaze toward Thalior, her heart heavy with the weight of their shared history. His face was a mask of anguish, his eyes darkened with the echoes of past pain. But beneath the surface, she could see the struggle. He was fighting something far more dangerous than the storm that raged around them.

"Selisyn," Thalior's voice broke through the roar of the winds, rough and strained, but with a resolve that chilled her. "I can't keep doing this. I can't keep dragging you through this endless cycle of pain. This—" He gestured to the tempest that surrounded them, "—this is our fate. This is the song. And it won't stop unless we make a choice."

His words landed like a weight on her chest, and she felt the ground beneath her feet shift. He was right, in a way. The cycle of love and loss, of passion and betrayal, had been repeating itself since the moment they had first met in this cursed realm. She had tried so hard to fight it, to break free of the pull that connected them. But the storm was showing her the truth— there was no escape. The song, their bond, had been twisted by forces beyond their comprehension, forces that had set them on a path they could never outrun.

"I won't let you do this alone," she whispered, her voice barely audible over the winds. Her eyes met his, and she saw the flicker of something deep within them—a fleeting moment of hope, a spark that had not yet been extinguished.

"You don't understand," he said, taking a step toward her. His hand reached for her, trembling as if the very act of touching her would shatter him. "The song has already taken so much from us. We can't keep living like this. If I break the bond, maybe… maybe you'll be free. Free of me. Free of this torment."

The words cut through her like a blade, sharp and unyielding. Free of him? How could he even say such a thing? Thalior was her heart, her soul, the only constant in a world that had always shifted beneath her feet. The thought of losing him, of being untethered from their connection, was unbearable.

"You don't get to decide that for me," Selisyn's voice rose, firm and filled with the fire of defiance. "This is not just your decision. We are in this together, for better or worse. You can't just cast me aside like some broken thing that needs fixing."

Thalior flinched, as if her words had struck him with the force of the storm itself. His eyes were wide, haunted by the shadows of their shared past. "I'm not casting you aside. I'm trying to protect you," he said, his voice cracking under the weight of his emotions. "I thought I could protect you by cutting us free. But every time I look at you, I see the hurt. I see the way this bond is breaking you, breaking us both."

His admission hit her like a blow to the chest. It wasn't just the storm that was tearing them apart—it was the unbearable truth of their past mistakes, the things they had done to each other, to themselves, and to the love they had once shared. She closed her eyes, letting the memory of the queen's betrayal flood back. The same betrayal that had been the catalyst for all of this. She had seen it once before, in the vision of her past life, and now the storm was forcing her to relive it once more.

The image of the queen, standing alone in her throne room, her face pale and cold, filled her mind. Thalior, standing before her, his expression filled with guilt and remorse. She had accused him of betrayal then, just as she had done so many times since. But now, in the heart of the storm, the full weight of her own actions, her own inability to trust, became clear. She had pushed him away, just as the queen had pushed Thalior away in their past lives.

"Thalior," she whispered, her voice trembling with the realization. "I failed you. Just as the queen failed you. I thought I could trust you, but I—"

"Stop," Thalior interrupted, his hand reaching out to her, his expression pained. "This is not just about what happened in the past. It's about what we've become now. We've been caught in a cycle of lies and mistrust. And every time we try to escape, we're dragged back in. The storm is only the beginning. If we don't make a choice, we'll keep repeating the same mistakes forever."

The storm howled around them, the winds rising in a crescendo of fury, as though the very elements were echoing the turmoil in their hearts. Selisyn's chest tightened with the weight of his words, the suffocating truth that had been building in the air between them. This wasn't just about their past lives; it was about who they were now, and what they had become. Love had twisted into something unrecognizable, a force that bound them in ways they couldn't comprehend. But now, standing at the edge of the abyss, they were faced with the ultimate question: Could they forgive each other, or would they be consumed by the past?

Thalior stepped closer, his eyes dark with anguish. "Selisyn," he said softly, "I've hurt you. I know that. I've failed you. But this bond… this bond between us, it's tearing us apart. If I don't sever it now, we'll both be lost forever."

His words echoed in the silence that followed, and Selisyn felt the storm around them pause, as if waiting for her to make a decision. The winds slowed, the thundering roar of the sky dying down, but the tension between them remained, thicker than the storm itself.

Selisyn's heart ached as she met his gaze. She could feel his pain, his anguish, and yet she couldn't bring herself to let him go. The idea of being severed from him, of losing the bond that had shaped their lives, was more terrifying than the storm that raged around them.

"No," she whispered, her voice steady despite the chaos around them. "I won't let you do this. Not like this."

"Selisyn…" Thalior's voice cracked, and she could see the agony in his eyes. "I love you. But if this bond is the reason we keep suffering, I have to let you go. I have to set you free."

The words were like a blade to her heart. She knew he was right, in a way. Their love, their bond, had been poisoned by the storm, by the lies and betrayals that had festered in the darkness of their past. But she couldn't give up. Not now. Not when they were so close to breaking free.

"No, Thalior," she said firmly. "I won't let you make that decision for me. I am willing to sacrifice everything—my past, my future—to save us. To save you. If I have to sever the bond, I will."

Thalior's eyes widened in shock, but before he could respond, the storm surged once more, its fury returning with a vengeance. The winds howled, the sky split with jagged bolts of lightning. The force of the tempest was no longer just the force of nature; it was the force of their love, their pain, their choices, colliding.

And in that moment, they both realized the truth—they could either break each other completely or find a way to heal. But it would come at a cost.

As the storm raged around them, Selisyn knew that the choice they faced was one that would change everything.

The question was no longer whether they could forgive each

other. It was whether they could forgive themselves.

The storm's fury grew with an intensity that made the ground beneath Selisyn's feet tremble. Each gust of wind seemed to carry whispers of the past, twisted and distorted by time. The heavens themselves were rebelling, their cries matching the chaos that swirled in Selisyn's heart. She couldn't shake the feeling that this moment—this decision—was one that would define them, one that would either break them apart for eternity or bind them in ways neither of them could predict.

Her hand trembled as it reached out to Thalior, but she forced herself to stay steady. The gusts were so fierce now that she felt like she might be torn from the earth itself. Yet, her resolve held firm. She wouldn't let him make this decision alone. Not after everything they had fought for.

"I won't let you sacrifice yourself, Thalior," she said, her voice breaking through the storm. "We can't keep running from our past, from the mistakes we've made. But that doesn't mean we have to end this. Not like this."

Thalior's face contorted with pain, his eyes wild as he glanced at her. The power of the storm was too great now, threatening to tear them apart, and yet there was something in his eyes—something raw and vulnerable—that made her heart ache. She knew he was trying to protect her. She knew he was fighting the pull of their shared history, the weight of their past, the fear that everything they had built together would collapse under the pressure of the song's power.

"I'm not running, Selisyn," he said, his words almost lost in the roar of the wind. "I'm trying to free us from this cycle. We can't keep living like this. The storm—it's only going to get worse. We can't stop it unless one of us makes the ultimate sacrifice."

His words sliced through her, a painful reminder of the gravity of their situation. The storm was no longer just a force of nature—it was a manifestation of the force that bound them, a force they had been trying to outrun since they first met. And now, they were standing at the edge, forced to make a choice that could destroy everything.

Thalior reached for her, his hand brushing against hers, but the wind ripped him away, pulling him back into the swirling vortex of chaos that had engulfed them both. Selisyn stumbled, struggling to keep her footing as the storm howled louder, its intensity reaching a fever pitch. The very air crackled with energy, as though the world was about to break in two.

For a moment, Selisyn was blinded by the storm, unable to see anything beyond the swirling blackness. She felt her pulse race, the ground beneath her feet slipping away, and then, in a flash of searing white light, she was plunged into a vision.

It was a vision of the past—of the queen, standing alone in her throne room, her face pale and drawn with the weight of a betrayal that had shattered everything she held dear. The vision shifted, and Selisyn saw Thalior, kneeling before the queen, his face filled with regret and remorse. He was trying to explain himself, to beg for forgiveness, but the queen could not—would not—hear him.

"I loved you," Thalior had said, his voice raw with emotion. "But I failed you, Selisyn. I failed us both."

The words echoed in Selisyn's mind, the weight of them pulling her deeper into the vision. She saw the queen's eyes, cold and unforgiving, as she turned away from Thalior, leaving him in the darkness of her rejection. The betrayal had been complete. It had torn them apart in that life, just as it threatened to tear them apart in this one.

The vision shifted again, and now it was Selisyn who was standing in a throne room, but this time, there was no Thalior by her side. She was alone, her crown heavy on her head, her heart broken by the very choices that had led her here. The song—the hollow song—echoed through the chamber, its melody a cruel reminder of the love she had lost, the love that had been twisted beyond recognition.

"You can't change the past," a voice whispered in her ear, and Selisyn whirled around, searching for the source of the words.

There, standing in the shadows, was Torianth Vallis, the ancient guardian they had encountered earlier. His eyes gleamed with an unsettling light, his form partially obscured by the storm that raged around them. He stepped forward, his voice carrying an eerie calmness amidst the chaos.

"This is the power of the song," Torianth said, his voice deep and resonant. "It bends time, shapes reality. You cannot escape what has been written, Selisyn. The bond you share with Thalior—it is more than just love. It is the foundation of this world, the tether that holds it together. But in your past, it was broken. And now, it threatens to break you both again."

Torianth's words sent a chill down her spine, and Selisyn felt herself drawn deeper into the vision, her thoughts swirling in a storm of confusion and fear. She was caught between two worlds—the past, where betrayal had shattered everything, and the present, where the song's power threatened to undo them once more.

"Is this our fate?" she asked, her voice trembling as the weight of the storm pressed down on her. "Are we doomed to repeat the same mistakes, over and over?"

Torianth's eyes softened, and for a brief moment, there

The Hollow Song of Eternity

was something almost sad in his gaze. "That is the question you must answer," he said. "The storm—the song—it is a manifestation of your deepest fears. It will show you the choices you made, the mistakes you've carried with you. But it is also an opportunity, a chance for you to break free. If you choose to confront the past, to forgive yourselves, you will break the cycle. If you choose to run, to continue in this endless loop of love and betrayal, you will remain trapped."

The storm intensified again, the winds howling louder as the dark skies seemed to crack open above them. The very air was alive with the power of the song, the echoes of a love that had been twisted by the forces of time. Selisyn felt herself pulled back into the present, her vision flickering as she looked once more at Thalior.

His face was contorted in anguish, his expression one of deep conflict. She could see the pain in his eyes, the torment of a love that had been tested to its limits. He was struggling, torn between his desire to protect her and the fear that the storm—the bond—would destroy them both.

"You have to choose, Selisyn," Thalior's voice broke through the storm, urgent and desperate. "We can't keep living like this. I can't keep hurting you. I love you, but I can't bear to see you suffer anymore."

The words shattered her heart, and for a moment, she didn't know if she could continue. The storm was closing in, the winds battering her from all sides, and yet, in that moment, she realized something—the love they had shared, the bond they had forged, was worth the sacrifice. It was worth fighting for.

"No," she said, her voice steady despite the chaos that surrounded them. "I won't let you go, Thalior. I won't let this song tear us apart. We've made mistakes, but we can still find a way to break the cycle. We can still choose love."

Torianth's words echoed in her mind as the storm raged on. **"You must forgive yourselves."**

Thalior's eyes locked with hers, and for a moment, the storm seemed to pause, as though the very world was holding its breath. He stepped toward her, his face filled with determination. The wind seemed to die down just enough for her to hear his voice, clear and strong.

"You're right," he said, his tone firm. "We can't let this song define us. We can't let it take away what we've fought for. We have one chance, Selisyn. One chance to break free."

And with that, they turned toward the heart of the storm, together. The final confrontation had begun, and their choices would determine whether their love would endure—or whether it would be lost forever.

Thirteen

The Wrath of the Song

The storm had reached its zenith, the world trembling beneath the weight of the song. The winds howled, a cacophony of shrieks and whispers that tore through the air, slicing into their minds like a thousand sharpened blades. Selisyn's heart pounded in her chest, her breath coming in short, jagged gasps as she clung to Thalior, struggling to stay grounded amidst the chaos.

Everything around them twisted. The sky warped into a swirling vortex of dark and light, pulling them into its grasp, the very fabric of reality beginning to tear apart as if the universe itself was unraveling. The song—the hollow song—was not just a melody now; it was a living thing, breathing, pulsing, growing, stretching out from the storm like a vast, all-encompassing entity, its haunting strains weaving into every corner of existence.

Thalior's grip tightened around her, his fingers digging into her skin as he fought against the onslaught. But it was no use. The power of the song was far too great, far too overwhelming. It seemed to be everywhere, in the air, in the ground, in the very blood that coursed through their veins.

And then, the song shifted.

It was no longer just a melody; it became something else, something darker, something... alive. The winds stilled for a brief moment, a pregnant silence settling over the world. Then, in the center of the storm, a figure began to form, glowing with an ethereal light that flickered like fire, casting strange, shifting shadows in its wake.

The entity that emerged was a being of contradictions—a being of both light and shadow, a silhouette of impossible grace and unfathomable power. Its form rippled, as though it were made of both solid matter and something intangible, something that existed beyond the realms of understanding. Its face, if it could be called a face, was both mesmerizing and terrifying, shifting between countless expressions in the span of a heartbeat, each one more foreign than the last.

The entity opened its mouth, and the melody—its song—poured forth, reverberating through the very air. The sound was no longer a mere tune. It was a force, an undeniable presence that pressed in on them from all sides, warping time, distorting space, bending the laws of reality until nothing made sense anymore.

The words it sang were ancient, incomprehensible—yet, as they reverberated in Selisyn's mind, she understood. The song was its very essence, and it was speaking to them, to her and Thalior, as though they were the only ones left in the world. Its voice was haunting, the melody an almost cruel lullaby.

"Selisyn. Thalior," the entity sang, its voice thick with

malevolent affection. "I am The Singularity. You are my creation, my masterpiece. The very bond that ties you—your love, your pain, your loss—is the foundation of this realm. Without you, there is nothing. Without you, the song cannot be sung, and the world... will collapse."

Selisyn's breath hitched in her throat. The words wrapped around her like chains, pulling at her, binding her to the entity with an invisible force she could not resist. The power it wielded was unlike anything she had ever known—unrelenting, all-consuming.

Thalior's voice cut through the oppressive silence, hoarse with emotion. "What do you want from us? Why are you doing this?"

The Singularity's form shifted again, its shape now a twisted blend of light and shadow that seemed to devour the world around it. "What I want is simple," it said, its voice a melody that twisted into something dark and cruel. "I want you to stay with me. Forever. Your love—your bond—is the music that sustains me. You cannot escape it. You cannot escape me. This world exists because of you. Without you, it would cease to be."

The song swelled, the melody rising to a fevered pitch, shaking the very foundations of reality. The ground beneath their feet cracked, splintering into jagged shards as the air hummed with an unbearable tension. Time itself seemed to warp, the seconds stretching into eternity, each moment a drawn-out echo of the last.

Selisyn felt herself being pulled toward the entity, the very essence of her being bending to the will of the song. It was as if the world was slipping away, as if she were no longer standing in reality but instead drifting through a void, disconnected from everything that had once been.

Thalior's hand tightened around hers, his grip unyielding. "Selisyn, don't—" His voice broke through the song's oppressive melody, but the words were drowned by the overwhelming force of the entity's presence.

They could feel it then—the truth that The Singularity had forced upon them, the horrifying realization that had been lurking at the edges of their consciousness all along. Their love, the very thing that had once felt so pure, so powerful, was now a weapon used against them. It was the thread that held the song together, and to break it would be to shatter the world they knew.

Selisyn's mind spun, the weight of the truth pressing down on her chest like a stone. The song—the entity—was not just manipulating them. It was feeding off them, using their love as a source of power, and if they broke the bond between them, if they severed the connection they shared, everything would cease to exist.

But if they stayed, they would be trapped forever, bound by the song's will, forced to replay their love, their loss, for eternity.

"What choice do we have?" she whispered, her voice cracking. Her eyes locked with Thalior's, and for the briefest of moments, she saw it—the same fear, the same desperation reflected in his gaze. But beneath it, there was something else: a fierce determination, a quiet resolve.

He pulled her closer, their bodies pressed together against the storm. "We fight," he said, his voice firm, despite the chaos swirling around them. "We fight for our love. We fight to break free."

The Singularity laughed then, the sound like a thousand

mournful echoes, rising above the storm, mocking them. "You think you can break free?" it taunted. "You think you can fight me? I am the song. I am the reason you exist. You cannot escape me."

The melody intensified, growing sharper, colder, each note a blade that sliced through their souls. Selisyn gasped, her body trembling as she felt the very core of her being being torn apart by the song. Every beat of her heart seemed to sync with the rhythm of the melody, and the pain—oh, the pain—was unbearable.

Thalior's voice rang out, clear and determined. "We will not be your prisoners. We will not live in this cycle of pain. We are not your creation. We are more than that."

The Singularity's form flickered, its light and shadow twisting together in a violent dance. The song grew louder, more insistent, until it was all-consuming. Selisyn could feel the very fabric of reality breaking around them, the edges of their existence fraying as the song's grip tightened.

She could feel it then—the presence of their love, pulsing in the very air between them, stronger than any force the entity could summon. It was their love that had brought them this far, their bond that had kept them together despite everything. It was the one thing the Singularity could not control.

Selisyn took a step forward, her eyes locked with Thalior's. They both understood now. Their love wasn't the key to their destruction. It was the key to their salvation. They had to use it, to make it their weapon, to shatter the song's hold over them.

With a final, defiant breath, Selisyn reached out, her hand trembling as she pressed it against the storm's heart. "Together," she whispered.

The Wrath of the Song

Thalior's hand joined hers, and the force of their connection surged through them, sending a shockwave through the storm. The song faltered, its melody stuttering for the first time, as if it were unsure of itself.

The Singularity roared in fury, but it was too late. The power of their love—the very force that had bound them together, that had created this realm—began to burn, blazing brighter than the light of the stars, hotter than the flames of the sun.

And as the storm began to collapse, as the fabric of reality tore apart, they knew: they had one chance. One chance to destroy the song, to break free from its grasp, and to forge a new path—together.

The haunting melody wrapped itself around them, thick and oppressive. It was a sound that sank deep into their bones, tugging at their very essence, as though the notes themselves were tearing at the fibers of their souls. The Singularity's form flickered, shifting between light and shadow, flickering like a dying flame on the verge of being snuffed out. Its voice echoed in their minds, reverberating with a power that seemed to twist the very fabric of reality.

"You don't understand, do you?" The Singularity's voice was a haunting whisper that curled into the spaces between Selisyn and Thalior's thoughts, cold and filled with an unsettling authority. "This love, this bond you share—it is the very foundation of this realm. Without it, the balance would collapse. You are the heart of this world."

Selisyn's breath hitched. She could feel the pressure of the song—its weight growing heavier, its sound louder, more suffocating, pressing against her chest until it felt as if her ribs would crack. She reached out instinctively to Thalior, her fingers brushing against his. His hand felt cold, his pulse erratic. They were both shaking, caught in the throes of the entity's power.

"Why?" Selisyn whispered, her voice strained, as she tried to resist the pull of the song. "Why are you doing this to us? We've done nothing to deserve this fate."

The Singularity's form flickered again, and for a fleeting moment, Selisyn saw something—*someone*—beneath the surface of the light and shadow. A figure, blurred and distant, like a memory she couldn't quite grasp. But then the vision vanished, and the creature's voice was back, louder, more triumphant.

"You are my creation," it purred. "Born from the deepest depths of love and despair. Your connection is eternal—your love has no equal. Do you think you can destroy that which you have created together?"

Thalior's jaw clenched. His chest heaved with each breath, and the weight of the Singularity's words crashed against him like a storm. It *was* their love that had formed the very foundation of this realm, that had birthed the song. But now, standing at the center of the storm, it seemed as though their love had become their curse.

"No," Thalior said, his voice hoarse. "We won't let you use us anymore. We won't be your puppets."

The Singularity's laugh was sharp, a jagged sound that cut through the air, like the tearing of paper. "You are already mine, Thalior. You always have been." The creature's form shifted again, its light intensifying until it felt as though the world itself was burning from the inside out. "And I will never let you go."

Selisyn could feel the strength of the bond between them, a pulsing force deep inside her. It had always been there, binding her to Thalior. But now, that same force seemed to pull at her in a way that hurt. It was as though the very heart of her was being torn apart, the love she shared with him turned into something *painful*—something that felt less like salvation and more like imprisonment.

"We have to stop this," she said, her voice trembling with the weight of her resolve.

Thalior nodded, though his expression was strained, the edges of his face tight with tension. "We have to fight back," he said, though the doubt that lingered in his voice betrayed the uncertainty in his heart.

The Singularity responded with a growl, its form swirling as if preparing to strike. "You cannot fight what is already inside you," it said, its words venomous. "Your love belongs to me now. And if you attempt to break free, you will lose everything. Your souls will be shattered, and your love will be forgotten."

A deep sense of dread bloomed inside Selisyn. Could the Singularity truly be right? Could they truly forget each other? The very thought made her heart ache, a sharp, raw feeling that almost felt like a physical wound. The idea of losing Thalior, of never remembering the depths of their connection, was too much to bear.

But as the Singularity's voice continued to twist through her mind, something deep within her stirred—a quiet, insistent thought. *They can't win. Not like this. We've already lost too much.*

Thalior stepped closer to her, his hand firm around hers, grounding her, even as the world around them seemed to tear apart. His eyes were filled with an emotion she couldn't quite place—grief? Regret? Determination? Perhaps all of them.

"This isn't just about us anymore," he said quietly, his gaze never leaving hers. "We have to stop the song. We have to free this realm from the darkness that's been feeding off our pain and love."

The weight of his words hit her like a wave, and for a brief moment, she was overcome by the magnitude of their task. The Singularity—the very force that had bound them together—was not just a force of love, but one that had been feeding off their suffering. It was the root of all the torment they'd faced, the reason they had been forced to repeat their love and loss in endless cycles. And now, with the storm raging around them, they had to make their final stand.

"We *can* do this," Selisyn said, her voice gaining strength. "We've come this far. And we're not going to let this thing take everything from us."

The Singularity's form rippled with anger, and for a moment, the light that had enveloped it flared with such intensity that it almost blinded them both. "You think you can defeat me?" The entity's voice was filled with contempt, but beneath the anger, there was a strange sense of fear. "I am the beginning and the end. I am the song, the creator, the keeper of your fate."

"Not anymore," Thalior said, his grip tightening around Selisyn's hand.

With that, he pulled her forward, stepping toward the swirling vortex of light and shadow that was the Singularity. The air around them thickened with pressure, the very atmosphere vibrating with the power of the entity. For a brief moment, it felt as though the world itself was holding its breath, as if time itself was waiting to see what would happen next.

And then, in a moment that felt like eternity, Thalior and Selisyn did something they hadn't done before. They didn't just fight against the song. They *embraced* it.

They pressed their hearts together, their minds and souls intertwining, their love acting as a weapon of its own. They poured everything they had into the bond—their hope, their pain, their fear, and above all, their love. As they did, the melody of the song began to shift, the notes bending and warping, no longer harmonious but twisted and strained, like a broken chord.

The Singularity screamed in frustration, its form shifting violently as it tried to push back against their power. But it was too late. The bond they had forged, their love, was no longer just a tool for the entity to wield. It had become the very weapon that would undo it.

With one final, unified effort, Thalior and Selisyn unleashed their love, shattering the song's hold over them, over the realm, and over the Singularity itself.

The song's final note echoed through the air, a single, discordant wail that seemed to reverberate through every fiber of their being. And then, there was silence.

Fourteen

The Final Choice

The air crackled with tension as the aftermath of the battle reverberated through the shattered landscape. Time itself seemed to twist and bend, the fabric of reality fraying at the edges like the remnants of an ancient tapestry. Selisyn and Thalior stood at the precipice, their bodies aching from the strain of the battle they had just fought. The ground beneath them was a fractured mosaic of light and shadow, the echoes of the Singularity's power still humming in the air. But there was no time to rest. The final choice awaited them.

The Singularity, once a towering and omnipotent force, was now a flickering wisp of light and shadow, trembling as if in the throes of death. The storm had dissipated, but the silence left in its wake was deafening. It was as though the entire world was holding its breath, waiting for something—anything—to happen.

The Final Choice

Thalior reached for Selisyn's hand, his fingers cold, his palm trembling against hers. His face was gaunt, his eyes wide and haunted, yet there was a fierceness in them now—something primal, something determined.

"This is it," he whispered, his voice hoarse. "We've done everything we can. But to destroy the song, one of us has to die."

Selisyn's heart clenched at his words. She knew it was true. She could feel it in the air—the weight of the decision pressing down on them, suffocating them. The very air around them seemed to pulse with the gravity of the moment. Her heart, however, refused to accept it. She had come this far, had fought alongside Thalior through trials and torment. They had defied the odds, faced darkness together. But now, the possibility that one of them had to die felt like a cruel twist of fate.

Thalior's gaze locked onto hers, and there was a desperation in his eyes that she had never seen before. "Selisyn, please," he said, his voice breaking. "I can't lose you. Not like this. You've already given so much. Let me be the one."

"No," she said, shaking her head fiercely, pulling her hand from his grasp. The thought of him sacrificing himself—of him dying to save her—was unbearable. She couldn't let him. Not after everything they had endured together.

"You don't understand," he continued, his voice trembling as his eyes searched hers, pleading for understanding. "This is the only way. You know it's true. If I die, the song will be destroyed, and you can go on with your life. You can find peace. I'll die knowing that you're free. That's all I want for you, Selisyn."

Her chest constricted as the weight of his words threatened to crush her. His selflessness—his willingness to lay down his life for her—was both the most beautiful and the most painful thing she had ever known. But she couldn't accept it. She wouldn't.

"No!" she cried again, her voice rising with desperation. "I won't let you do this. I *won't* lose you. You don't have to make this sacrifice."

Thalior took a step back, his face contorting with a mixture of frustration and sorrow. "You don't get it, Selisyn," he said, his voice tight with emotion. "I've already lost you. I lost you long ago. You are bound to this song. To the Singularity. There's no escaping it. If one of us doesn't make this choice, we'll both be consumed. We'll both lose everything."

Selisyn felt a pang deep within her chest, a sharp, painful realization. Thalior was right. The love they shared, the bond that had sustained them through everything, had been tainted by the very song they had fought to destroy. It was like a poison in their veins, slowly eroding everything they held dear. She had always feared this moment—the moment when their love would either save them or tear them apart. And now, here it was.

"I won't live without you, Thalior," she whispered, her voice barely a breath, her heart breaking with the weight of the truth she had always known. "I can't."

For a long moment, neither of them spoke. The world around them seemed to hold its breath, as if the universe itself were waiting for the outcome of their choices.

Then, suddenly, the Singularity's voice echoed through the air, its once-mighty presence now a faint whisper, but still powerful enough to send a chill down their spines.

"You are foolish," the entity intoned, its voice like the wind, soft yet filled with malice. "You think your love is enough to defy me? You think that sacrifice—*any* sacrifice—will free you from the bonds I've placed upon you?"

Selisyn's breath caught in her throat, and Thalior instinctively reached for her, pulling her close. The Singularity's presence seemed to grow stronger, the shadows of its form swirling ominously. "You've already done enough," it continued, its voice growing louder, more insistent. "Your love is mine. And you will *never* escape it."

Selisyn felt the weight of its words pressing down on her chest. The song's power was suffocating, wrapping itself around her like a noose, pulling at the very core of her being. The entity had a point—they had already lost so much. Their love had already been warped by the power of the song, had already been twisted into something they no longer recognized. But still, they had fought for it. They had fought for each other. And now, the decision lay in their hands.

"Do you really think your love can destroy me?" The Singularity's voice laughed, a hollow, chilling sound that echoed through the air. "You're wrong. I will offer you one final choice—live without your love, or die with it. The price is steep, but it is the only way."

The words hit them like a thunderclap, a crack of lightning that split the sky. Selisyn and Thalior both froze, their minds reeling at the gravity of what the Singularity had just offered. The entity's form flickered again, casting a shadow across them both, its voice now cold and unyielding.

"I will allow you to live," it continued, "but you must give up the one thing that binds you together. Your love. Forget each other. Erase the bond you've forged, and you will be free. But if you refuse... if you continue to resist... one of you must die."

The offer hung in the air, suspended between them like a

dark promise. For a moment, Selisyn couldn't breathe. The weight of the choice crushed her, her mind spinning. Could they really live without each other? Could they really forget everything they had shared—the passion, the love, the agony, the joy?

Thalior's voice broke through her thoughts, quiet but resolute. "We can't lose each other, Selisyn. We've come too far."

Selisyn looked at him, her heart breaking. The love they shared was a force unlike any other. But could it survive the ultimate sacrifice? Could they truly *forget* each other, erase the bond that had defined them for so long?

And so, as the Singularity's presence loomed larger, and the storm of choices raged around them, they stood on the precipice of a final decision—one that would change everything.

The air grew colder as the Singularity's presence pressed down on them, suffocating every thought, every whisper of defiance. The offer was clear—live without their love, or perish with it. The weight of the decision crushed them both. The choice was agonizing, and every part of Selisyn's being screamed to hold onto the love she and Thalior had fought so hard for. But the Singularity's words echoed in her mind, drowning out all other thoughts.

Thalior stepped closer to her, his eyes searching her face with a tenderness that made her heart ache. His voice was soft but unwavering. "We can't let this destroy us, Selisyn. We have to choose. We've already sacrificed so much, but this…" He shook his head, the words nearly impossible for him to say. "I can't live with the thought that you'll die because of me. I'll do anything. If it means erasing our love, I will let it go."

The Final Choice

Selisyn felt the tears well up, blurring her vision. No matter how much she tried to resist the emotion, the reality of what he was offering tore at her insides. Her heart ached for him, for her, for the love they had built. To live without each other—to forget everything they had endured together—was an impossible thought. It was a fate worse than death. She couldn't let that happen. Not now, not after everything they had sacrificed to get here.

"No, Thalior," she choked out, her voice trembling with the weight of her decision. "I won't let you be the one to make that choice. Not for me. Not when it's my life that I am willing to give. You've given me everything already. I won't take any more from you."

He stepped back, his expression haunted, as if he had already accepted the burden of her words, but the struggle was written clearly across his face. The tension between them was palpable, thick with grief and love, both impossible to reconcile.

The Singularity's voice rang out again, this time more insistent, mocking. "You are fools. You are *already* bound to me. You will *never* be free of me, no matter what choice you make. If you think you can escape the song, you are deluding yourselves. I will always be a part of you."

Selisyn turned, her eyes narrowing with defiance as she faced the flickering form of the Singularity. "We're not yours," she said, her voice low but steady. "We're not bound by you any longer. We're choosing our own fate."

The shadows in the Singularity's form writhed in response, the entity's presence twisting as if in fury. "You have no power here, Selisyn. None of you do. The song will remain. The love you feel, the bond you share, it is mine to control."

But as it spoke, Selisyn noticed something. The air around

them seemed to vibrate, a tremor running through the very ground, and for a moment, the Singularity faltered. The bond that had connected them to the song, the pull it had exerted on their souls, seemed to weaken. Just slightly, but enough to give her hope.

"Thalior," she whispered urgently, turning back to him. "There's a chance… We can fight it. We can break free. But we have to make the choice—together. You have to trust me."

Thalior's eyes widened, and for a moment, he looked like he might argue, to reject her words. But the look in her eyes—the fierceness of her resolve—melted something inside him. He had always trusted her, always believed in the bond between them.

"Together," he said, his voice thick with emotion. "Always."

The Singularity seemed to sense the shift in the air, and its form grew darker, more menacing. "You will regret this," it spat, its voice a shrill screech, like nails on glass. "You *cannot* break free. I am your creator, your keeper. Without me, you are nothing."

The ground beneath them trembled, and suddenly, the skies overhead cracked open, lightning flashing through the jagged seams in the world. A storm of light and shadow swirled violently above, casting long, twisted shadows over Selisyn and Thalior. The air grew thick with the pulse of the song—louder now, echoing through the very core of their beings.

Selisyn reached for Thalior's hand again, her fingers wrapping tightly around his. The bond between them, the connection that had been both their greatest strength and their greatest burden, was now their weapon. Together, they could tear through the veil that had trapped them in this song. They had been bound to the song for so long, but now they would choose to break it.

"I will not live without you," she whispered, her voice barely audible over the roar of the storm. "And I won't let you live without me."

Thalior looked at her, his eyes dark with sorrow and resolve. "Then we fight. Together." His voice was firm now, filled with the strength of their shared love, their shared determination.

The storm above them swirled faster, its winds howling with the fury of the Singularity's power. The very fabric of reality bent, twisting, warping, as if the world itself was being torn apart. But through it all, Selisyn and Thalior stood firm, locked in a bond that nothing, not even the Singularity itself, could break.

The Singularity's voice echoed again, louder this time, reverberating through their souls. "You are nothing without me! You will *never* escape me!"

The words sent a shiver of fear through Selisyn, but she refused to let it take hold. She drew on the strength of the love that had always defined her and Thalior's relationship. She had fought for it. She had lived for it. And now, she would die for it if she had to.

"Not without each other," she said, her voice filled with unwavering conviction. "You can't take what you didn't create."

The Singularity's form flickered violently, as if caught in a storm of its own making. The winds howled louder, the skies crackling with energy. Time itself seemed to fracture around them, pulling them in all directions. The very foundation of the realm trembled, as though it, too, could feel the strain of their defiance.

Then, in a flash of light, the Singularity's presence surged toward them, a blinding explosion of light and shadow. Selisyn felt herself being pulled into the storm, her body twisting as if the very air was trying to tear her apart. The last thing she saw before everything went black was Thalior's face—his eyes locked on hers, filled with determination, with love.

And then, the storm exploded into pure, searing light.

Fifteen

The Cost of Time

The light was blinding. Selisyn's vision blurred, then darkened completely, as though the world itself was being erased. She gasped for air, as if her lungs could not hold the weight of her own breath. It felt as though she was falling through an endless chasm, the world cracking apart around her.

The storm, the Singularity, Thalior... everything dissolved into nothingness. No more shadows, no more voices, no more haunting melodies. Just silence—pure, suffocating silence.

But then, slowly, the darkness receded, and the world began to form once more, but not as it had been. The ground beneath her feet was soft and foreign, like nothing she had ever felt. The sky above stretched in a wash of muted grays, heavy clouds swirling in disarray. No sun. No stars. Just the deep, oppressive stillness of a world that had lost its heartbeat.

"Thalior?"

Her voice trembled as it echoed across the desolate landscape. She turned, the silence pressing against her like a suffocating force. There was no answer.

She blinked rapidly, searching the barren horizon, her pulse racing in her ears. Had the world collapsed completely? Had they been erased from existence?

Then, as if pulled from the very fabric of her thoughts, a figure appeared in the distance. Tall, broad-shouldered, his presence unmistakable. Thalior.

But something was wrong. He was moving slowly, almost as if walking through treacle, and there was a blankness to his expression, a fog in his eyes. His gaze didn't land on her. He passed by, his steps heavy, as though he could not see her, hear her, or remember her.

"Thalior?" she whispered again, her voice barely a breath. The words felt foreign in her mouth, but they carried the weight of her entire existence.

He continued forward, unaffected, lost in the haze of the world around him. She reached out instinctively, but her hand passed through him as if he were nothing more than a shadow, an illusion.

Her heart hammered in her chest, a painful rhythm that made her breath catch. She stumbled back, disoriented, trying to ground herself, to make sense of what was happening. This couldn't be real. She could still feel the echo of him inside her, the love, the bond that had shaped everything they had been. How could he be there but not *there*? How could she *feel* him so deeply, yet see him as if he were a stranger?

And then, as if the world had been holding its breath, the Singularity's voice pierced through the silence, hollow and cold.

"Do you see now, Selisyn? Do you understand the price of freedom?"

The voice echoed from all directions, vibrating through her very bones. Selisyn's knees buckled beneath her, the reality of the situation hitting her with a force that made her gasp. She pressed her hands to her ears, trying to block out the sound, but it penetrated her mind, relentless and unforgiving.

"Your love was never truly yours. It was a creation, an illusion born from time itself. And now that time has fractured, it will erase what you were, what you *are*. No more love. No more memories. No more Thalior."

Selisyn's heart seemed to shatter in her chest as the words settled over her like a cold shroud. She wanted to scream, to rage, to demand that it be undone, that she *not* forget him, that she *not* lose him.

But she knew, deep down, that the choice had already been made. The cost had been paid.

The Singularity was offering them freedom, yes. But at what cost? The bond between them, the memories, the love—they were being erased. A clean slate. An ending. A new beginning.

And she could feel it, like the final thread of their connection snapping between them. The deep, unbreakable connection they had shared for so long was beginning to unravel, fading as the world around them crumbled.

Thalior's form grew more distant, more intangible, his presence slipping away from her grasp. Her heart ached with a loss so profound, it felt as though her very soul was being torn apart.

She could *feel* the absence of him, like a hollow echo within her. Every step she took seemed to distance her from him even more, each movement growing more sluggish, as though her body was losing its will, its purpose. The memory of him, once so vivid, was starting to blur, the edges becoming indistinct, faded like a dream slipping through her fingers.

A wave of dizziness washed over her. Her knees threatened to buckle once more as the ground seemed to shift beneath her feet. She reached out, clutching at the air, but the weight of the world pressed down on her, as if gravity itself were trying to drag her into oblivion.

The Singularity spoke again, its voice now more insistent, as though it reveled in her torment.

"Do you understand now, Selisyn? This is your reward—freedom from the burden of love, from the entanglement of time. You will walk away from this place, but you will walk alone."

Selisyn's body trembled as her mind reeled, the reality of the situation sinking in. She had chosen this. They had chosen this. Thalior's sacrifice had been the key, and now the price was being paid in full.

Her heart seemed to thud painfully against her ribs, but she couldn't *feel* him anymore. The connection they had shared, once so vibrant and all-encompassing, was now nothing more than an empty ache. The warmth of his touch, the sound of his voice—gone.

She turned slowly, her legs barely able to hold her, and began to walk toward the broken horizon, the world crumbling behind her. She couldn't look back. She couldn't let herself.

And yet, she felt a pull, a whisper of something still inside her—a deep, unrelenting desire to remember him, to *cling* to the last vestige of their shared history. It was all she had left.

But as she moved forward, the ground beneath her seemed to shift, as though the realm was breaking apart even faster

The Cost of Time

now, as if her every step was accelerating its collapse. The world was falling, not into chaos, but into *nothingness*.

She could feel the weight of her decision sinking deeper with each passing moment. The memories of Thalior were slipping further away, lost like fragments of a shattered glass that no one could ever piece together again.

Her footsteps slowed as the last of the light dimmed. The echo of her name—Thalior's name—died away in her mind, fading until it was nothing more than a whisper in the void.

And then, just as the final memory slipped from her grasp, she heard it. His voice.

"Selisyn."

Her heart stopped. For the briefest moment, the weight of the world lifted. Time seemed to stretch, warping and bending, the silence amplifying that one single word.

"Selisyn."

His voice. Thalior's voice.

She froze. Her breath caught in her throat as the sound of her name reverberated in the emptiness, a lifeline in the midst of the void. She turned, her eyes wild, searching the expanse. Her mind screamed for her to reach out, but her body remained still, trapped by the impossibility of it all.

There—beneath the darkened sky—he was. Thalior.

He stood there, barely more than a silhouette against the crumbling horizon, but he was there. His presence was faint, just a flicker in the distance, but the connection between them, the bond that had once been as strong as steel, pulled her forward, urging her to take that step, to close the gap that now existed between them.

But she didn't move. She couldn't. The pain of knowing he

was there but *not* there kept her rooted to the spot, her limbs heavy as if they were made of stone. Her heart pounded in her chest, so loud she feared it would drown out everything else.

"Thalior," she whispered again, her voice trembling. But it was no use. His form remained unchanged, a faint outline that refused to come any closer.

"Selisyn…"

The whisper of his voice cut through the silence once more, carrying with it the weight of their shared past. Her hands shook as she stepped forward, uncertain, her every movement slow and deliberate, as if the very air around her resisted her touch. But still, she moved, despite the ever-deepening sense of despair clawing at her from every direction.

With each step, the world seemed to shift again. Time itself seemed uncertain, slipping away from her grasp like water through her fingers. The ground beneath her feet felt soft, like sand. The edges of her perception frayed, like a dream beginning to fade before she could capture its full essence.

And yet—there he was.

"Thalior," she said again, this time louder, desperation leaking into her voice.

Finally, she took another step. Then another. And yet, no matter how much she moved, it seemed that the distance between them remained the same. She could feel him. She *knew* he was real, that he was there. But the world itself had betrayed her, had pulled them apart in ways she couldn't understand.

Then, as though the very air had thickened, a strange sensation swept over her—a dizzying sense of vertigo—as if she were teetering on the edge of a precipice, and just one wrong move would send her plummeting into the abyss.

A cold wind stirred the silence. The hairs on the back of her neck rose.

"Selisyn."

Her heart fluttered in her chest. His voice—stronger now, closer. But still... so far away.

She pressed forward, more urgently now, as the strange feeling that something was wrong intensified.

"Thalior! Please, I—I can't lose you!" Her voice cracked with the weight of the emotions she could no longer suppress. She was so close now—so close that she could feel the faintest warmth of his presence.

But then, with a suddenness that made her stumble, she stopped. Her heart stopped. Her breath caught.

The world had shifted once again.

Now, standing before her, Thalior—*no*... not Thalior—was an unfamiliar figure. The silhouette had sharpened into a vague shadow, more twisted than she remembered. His eyes—where once there had been light, warmth—were now vacant, hollow. They stared past her, through her, unseeing.

She gasped, stumbling back. The ground beneath her feet was now slick, unnaturally smooth. It was like walking on ice, and with every step, the void crept closer.

"No," she whispered, but her voice was shaky. "No, this isn't you. Thalior!"

But the figure before her remained still, its gaze fixed on some point beyond her reach, beyond time itself.

"I am no longer Thalior," the figure spoke in a voice that was not his. It was colder. Unfeeling. "I am what you have made me. A shadow of what could have been."

Selisyn's chest tightened. "This isn't real. You *are* him. You *have* to be him."

The shadow before her seemed to shift again, its form wavering like a mirage. The light around them flickered, blurring as time itself fractured again. Reality trembled.

"No," the shadow said softly, and in that one word, Selisyn could hear the echoes of everything they had been through, every whisper of love they had shared, every battle fought, every promise broken. "I am not him. Not anymore. You cannot bring him back."

The words struck like a dagger to her heart. She opened her mouth to speak, but no words came. She could only stare, her gaze fixed on the shadow before her, helpless, unable to comprehend what had happened, how it had all unraveled so completely.

"You," the shadow continued, its voice softer now, almost as though it pitied her, "have made your choice. You and Thalior—your love was a lie, a creation. And now it is gone. No memory of it remains."

"No," she whispered, the word barely escaping her lips as she shook her head, trying to dispel the impossible reality. "No! Please! Please—tell me it's not true! We—*we*—had love, had *life* together! You can't take it from me, from us!"

The shadow's lips twisted into a bitter semblance of a smile.

"You had a fleeting moment, a fragile thread. And now you must let go. The song has broken you both."

Tears welled in Selisyn's eyes, and before she could stop herself, they began to spill over, streaming down her face like silent rivers. Every tear seemed to carry away a piece of her heart, a piece of her soul, until there was nothing left but the hollow emptiness of what had been lost.

"Why?" she choked out, her voice trembling with pain. "Why can't we—why can't I—keep him? We *deserve* this. We *deserve* each other."

But the shadow only shook its head, its hollow eyes still locked onto hers.

"Deserve?" It laughed bitterly, and the sound sent a chill through her. "You have been deceived. What you sought to preserve, what you fought for… It is but a fragment of a time that should never have existed. The price of your love was paid long ago."

Selisyn felt the weight of the words sink deep into her, like an anchor pulling her to the depths. She wanted to scream, to rage, to tear everything apart, but she had no strength left. The tears fell faster, as if her very soul were breaking into pieces.

"You will remember," the shadow said, its voice barely a whisper now, "but you will remember nothing of him. Nothing of your love. Nothing of *this*."

And just like that, the shadow began to fade, the edges of its form dissipating into the void like dust in the wind. Her heart shattered in a thousand pieces as the darkness crept over her once again.

Sixteen

The Silent Song

The air was thick with a sense of unfamiliarity, like a heavy fog that clouded the mind, distorting even the most mundane of moments. Selisyn stood at the edge of a crowded market square, her gaze drifting over the faces of strangers. She had always been one to observe, to study the world around her in silence, but today, there was something different—something off.

It was the way the world seemed to pulse with an undercurrent of energy that she couldn't quite grasp. The vibrant stalls with their colorful wares, the laughter and chatter of the people—it all felt... muted, like a symphony without its melody. She walked through it, moving like a specter, her feet following a path she didn't remember setting.

Her heart thudded in her chest, a rhythm that felt too fast, too out of sync with her surroundings. There was a tug, a faint pull deep within her, a sensation she had experienced before but

The Silent Song

couldn't place. It was as though someone—something—was calling her name from the distance, but when she turned, no one was there.

She shook her head, trying to dispel the thought. The market was busy, people going about their lives, and yet the space around her seemed empty, hollow. She could feel the weight of the silence pressing in, and the urge to leave, to escape the crushing feeling, was almost overwhelming. But where would she go?

Her feet carried her forward, despite the wariness clawing at her chest. She passed a stall selling trinkets, the metal bells hanging from its eaves catching the sunlight and ringing in soft chimes. The sound should have been pleasant, but it struck her as wrong—out of place, as if the chimes were calling her, pulling her deeper into something she couldn't understand.

She reached out, almost instinctively, fingers brushing against the soft edges of a silver pendant. Her breath caught in her throat as a sharp, unfamiliar wave of recognition swept over her. A memory—no, a feeling—flashed in her mind, something she couldn't quite catch, a connection that was fleeting, like the last notes of a song disappearing into the void.

"Excuse me, miss," a voice interrupted, pulling her from the reverie. She turned to find a merchant staring at her, his brow furrowed with concern. "You're alright? You look like you've seen a ghost."

Selisyn blinked, shaking off the strange sensation. She gave him a small, tight smile. "I'm fine. Just a bit... distracted."

"Distracted?" The merchant grinned, his eyes glinting. "You've been staring at that pendant for a long time. Might be something to do with it, eh?"

Her gaze fell to the silver pendant once more, the cool metal glinting in the light. Something stirred within her, something deeply buried, but when she reached out to pick it up, the memory slipped away like water through her fingers. It was gone.

"No," she murmured, pulling her hand back, "I don't think so."

She walked away quickly, the unease growing inside her. The pull—the tug at her heart—was stronger now, more insistent. But what was it? And why did it feel like something she should remember? She had never seen that pendant before. Or had she?

The crowd shifted around her, but her thoughts spiraled, chasing after the echo of something that felt too distant to grasp. She needed to get away, to clear her head, but there was no place that felt safe, no place that felt like her own anymore. The world was different now. The song was silent, but the hollow echo lingered, gnawing at the edges of her consciousness.

She turned a corner and found herself alone, tucked away in a small, quiet alley, where the bustle of the market seemed a lifetime away. The sound of her own breath filled her ears, the only constant in the overwhelming silence. Her hand instinctively moved to her chest, where a strange, aching sensation throbbed deep inside, an emptiness that had no name.

And then, she felt it again. That tug. That presence.

Her heart skipped a beat as she spun around, eyes scanning the empty street. For a fleeting moment, she thought she saw him. Thalior. His figure—dark, shadowed, and distant—loomed just out of reach, his outline obscured by the shifting light. But when she blinked, the vision vanished, like a whisper

The Silent Song

in the wind.

"Thalior," she breathed, the name slipping from her lips before she could stop it.

But he wasn't there.

Her chest tightened, the pain of the lost connection surging up like a wave crashing against the shore. She closed her eyes, her breath shallow, as if by doing so she could force the memory to return. But there was nothing. No voice. No presence. Only the cold, empty silence.

Thalior sat on a stone bench at the edge of the same market square, watching the world pass him by in a blur of movement and noise. His hands rested on his knees, his fingers twitching with an unspoken restlessness. The market was the same as it always had been: vibrant, full of life, a place of motion and sound. But for him, it was as though the world was muted, a strange distortion in every interaction, every passing face.

It was hard to explain the way it felt. It was like an absence, a hole in his chest where something—or someone—had once been. He could feel it now, that pull. A presence just beyond his reach. He didn't know what it was, but he couldn't shake the feeling that something was missing. Something vital.

He glanced at the crowd, at the people moving around him, but his gaze always returned to the same place—the center of the square, where the sun was just beginning to dip low in the sky. It was then, amidst the sea of strangers, that he saw her.

Selisyn.

She was standing near a stall, her back to him, her eyes fixed on something in the distance. Her figure was a ghost, just out of reach. But it was her. He was certain of it.

His heart stuttered. The pull was stronger now, an invisible thread that bound him to her even though he didn't understand why. He had no memory of their past, no memory of who she was or what they had been. But standing there, in that moment, something deep inside him stirred, a flicker of recognition.

She moved, and instinctively, Thalior stood, his feet carrying him toward her without conscious thought. But with every step he took, the distance between them remained the same. She was walking, but not toward him. She seemed... lost, as if something was gnawing at her, pulling her in every direction.

"Selisyn," he whispered, the name slipping from his lips before he could think.

But she didn't hear him.

The tug in his chest tightened, and he took another step. But this time, something changed. She stopped. Her body went rigid, her gaze snapping to the side as though she had felt him there. But when she turned, her eyes met his, and for a moment, everything froze. Time seemed to hold its breath, and for the first time, he saw it—the spark of recognition in her eyes.

Her breath hitched, and for the briefest moment, Thalior thought he saw a flicker of hope there. But it was gone before it could settle, replaced by confusion, uncertainty.

Her lips parted as though she wanted to say something, but no words came. The silence between them felt thick, pressing against his chest, suffocating.

And then, just as quickly as it had come, the connection broke. She turned away, her steps quickening as she vanished into the crowd.

Thalior stood there, frozen, watching her go. His heart ached in his chest, but he couldn't explain why. Why did her absence feel like a knife lodged deep within him?

He wanted to follow her. He wanted to run, to shout, to tell her something—anything. But he didn't know what. And so, instead, he stood still, staring at the place where she had been, his mind spinning with unanswered questions.

What was it? What was the pull? And why was it so strong? And more importantly…

Who was she?

Selisyn's footsteps echoed in the empty alley, each one sharper than the last as if the world itself was pressing her forward, urging her to leave behind the haunting presence that clung to her like a shadow. She didn't look back. She couldn't. The ache in her chest was too raw, too consuming, and the more she thought about the brief moment when their eyes had locked, the more the confusion tightened its grip on her heart.

Who was he?

Why did his presence feel like a call to something buried deep inside her, something long forgotten?

Her breath came in shallow bursts as she walked faster, her mind reeling, trying to process the flood of emotions that threatened to break through the wall she had built around her heart. But nothing made sense. It was as though she was caught in a dream, a waking nightmare where everything was just out of reach, floating between reality and some distant, unreachable place.

She turned another corner, this time coming to a street she didn't recognize. The buildings were unfamiliar, old and weathered, as though the world itself had begun to forget its own history. She paused, her breath coming in quick, uneven bursts. The streets were eerily silent, save for the occasional flutter of wind through the trees. The weight of everything pressed in on her—the silence, the uncertainty, the feeling that something was slipping through her fingers, something she was desperately trying to hold onto.

Suddenly, a gust of wind swept through the alley, carrying with it a faint whisper, like a melody caught on the breeze. Her heart skipped, and she stopped dead in her tracks, her eyes scanning the narrow street as though searching for the source of the sound.

But there was nothing.

Nothing but the wind.

And yet, the pull in her chest remained.

It was as though a part of her was missing, something vital that had once been there, and now, she was left with only a hollow ache where it should have been. It was a feeling she couldn't explain, a gnawing emptiness that felt far too familiar, even though she couldn't place it.

The whisper came again, this time clearer, like the distant echo of a song, soft and haunting, drifting through the quiet streets. Her eyes narrowed as she tried to focus, tried to make sense of the melody that tugged at her very soul.

It was a song she knew. A song that had once filled her heart with warmth, with a sense of belonging.

A song that felt like it had been erased from her memory.

She took a step forward, moving toward the sound, each step bringing her closer to something, though she couldn't say what. The air around her seemed to shimmer, vibrating with an energy that was both soothing and unsettling. It was as if the world itself was trying to tell her something, trying to lead her somewhere, but she couldn't understand what it was, or why it was so important.

The further she walked, the more the song grew, filling her ears with its eerie, almost sorrowful melody. It was a tune she had once known by heart, a song she had once sung along with, and yet it now seemed like a memory just out of reach.

A memory she couldn't hold onto.

She turned the corner and froze.

In front of her, standing as though he had always been there, was Thalior. His figure was barely illuminated by the dim light of the setting sun, his dark silhouette a stark contrast to the glow of the fading day. He stood motionless, his eyes locked on her, the silence between them stretching out like an eternity.

The world seemed to pause. The song faded, swallowed by the heaviness of the moment.

"Thalior," Selisyn whispered, her voice breaking the stillness, though it felt like the word had been torn from her throat against her will. She took a hesitant step forward, and then another, as though she couldn't stop herself. Her heart raced, her breath quickening, and she didn't know why. She just knew that she had to be near him.

He didn't move, but his gaze never wavered. He stared at her with an intensity that felt like a physical force, his eyes dark and filled with something—something she couldn't quite place. Recognition? Longing? Or perhaps something else altogether.

For a long moment, neither of them spoke. The wind whispered around them, but the world felt so quiet, so still, that it seemed as if everything else had faded into the background.

And then, at last, Thalior spoke, his voice low, almost hesitant.

"I... I don't know why, but I feel like I should know you."

His words struck her like a blow, a sharp pain that lanced through her chest. The ache deep inside her flared, and she clenched her fists, her nails digging into her palms as if to ground herself.

"I feel it too," Selisyn murmured, barely able to speak over the rush of emotions flooding her. "But I don't remember you."

The words left her mouth before she could stop them, and as soon as they were spoken, the reality of what they meant sank in like a stone in her gut. She didn't remember him.

But that wasn't the worst part.

The worst part was that she knew she should. She should remember him. The pull, the ache, everything inside her told her that they had been something—someone—important to each other.

But now... nothing.

The silence between them stretched out again, thick with tension. Neither of them knew what to say, and yet, it felt like there was so much they both needed to say. It was as if the silence was too heavy to bear, the weight of everything unsaid pressing down on them both.

Selisyn opened her mouth to speak, to ask him what was happening, to try to make sense of the chaos inside her. But before she could, the song returned.

It was faint at first, like a whisper on the wind, but it grew louder with each passing second. The melody swirled around them, familiar yet foreign, its notes twisting in a way that made her heart ache.

It was the same song.

The song that had once filled the air between them, a song of their love, their shared history.

And yet... there was something wrong with it now.

The melody, once sweet and full of promise, now carried a hint of sorrow. A sorrow that weighed down on Selisyn's heart like a thousand unspoken words. She could feel it—the loss, the emptiness, the absence of something she couldn't define.

The Silent Song

The song pulsed around her, wrapping her in its haunting embrace.

And then, a voice—soft, almost too soft to hear—spoke from the shadows.

"The song is still inside you, Selisyn. The song will always be inside you."

She froze, her heart lurching in her chest. The voice—there was no mistaking it. It was the same voice that had whispered to her from the very beginning, the one that had guided her through the realm, through time.

The same voice that had promised her love, but at a cost.

Selisyn's hand shot out, grabbing Thalior's arm as the world around them seemed to tilt, the ground beneath their feet shifting as though reality itself was beginning to unravel.

"Thalior… What's happening?" she gasped, her voice trembling with the weight of everything that was crashing down around her.

The song—his voice—was the only thing she could hear now. It was the only thing she could feel.

And it was pulling her, dragging her into the darkness.

Seventeen

Echoes of Love

The wind was colder now, the kind that sliced through skin and bone with a quiet, relentless determination. The sky above Selisyn was a swirling mass of dark clouds, bruised and pregnant with the weight of an approaching storm. Yet, amidst the threatening weather, a strange stillness settled over the city—a stillness that felt both comforting and unnerving.

Selisyn walked through the streets, her feet carrying her with a purpose she didn't quite understand. She had been walking for hours, or maybe days—it was difficult to track time when everything felt out of place. The city around her seemed foreign, the buildings more twisted than she remembered, their shadows stretching unnaturally across the ground, as though the very fabric of reality had begun to warp.

And yet, she couldn't shake the feeling that she wasn't alone. Her heart thudded in her chest, the rhythm matching

Echoes of Love

the pulse of something deep within her—something old, something forgotten, something that whispered to her in the quiet moments. A song. It was always there, swirling beneath the surface of her thoughts, lingering in the corners of her mind like a half-remembered dream. A melody that both comforted and tormented her, pulling at her very soul.

She stopped in the middle of the street, her breath misting in the air. Her eyes scanned the crowd, though it was sparse, and her mind was only half-aware of the people walking past. The faces were blurry, the colors muted, like everything was being seen through a fogged lens.

But then… there was a presence. It was a subtle shift in the air, the faintest pressure at the back of her neck. Something—or someone—was watching her.

Her heart skipped a beat.

She didn't know why, but she felt it. The pull. The connection. It was a silent force, an echo of something deeper, something that tugged at her with a force that felt both familiar and foreign.

It was him.

Thalior.

Selisyn's breath caught in her throat, her fingers trembling as she reached out, instinctively, toward the familiar presence that seemed to draw her in. But when her eyes searched the crowd, she saw nothing.

He wasn't here. Not in the way she had hoped.

Still, the sensation remained, gnawing at her. That sense of him. Of *something* she couldn't quite define.

She forced herself to move again, her feet taking her through the streets, though every step felt heavy, as though she was walking against an invisible current.

And then, suddenly, a soft sound broke through the haze.

A whisper of a song.

It was faint, at first—a flutter on the edge of hearing, as if carried by the wind itself. The melody wrapped around her, soothing her with a bittersweet tenderness. The tune was so familiar, so *alive*, that Selisyn's chest tightened in response.

The song.

It was the song.

She stopped again, her hands pressed to her chest as she tried to steady her breathing. The song tugged at her heart, pulling her toward it, toward *him*.

A shadow passed by her in the street, and for a brief moment, she could have sworn she saw a figure that felt... familiar. Someone tall, with dark, tousled hair and a presence that resonated deep within her.

Her heart stuttered, and she turned her head, her eyes following the man as he walked away.

There was something about him.

She couldn't place it—couldn't even define it—but she felt it in her bones. He was a memory just out of reach, a flicker in the back of her mind.

She hesitated.

It was foolish, she knew. She had no reason to chase after a stranger in the middle of a city that seemed to have forgotten its own name. But the pull, the connection—it was undeniable. It was like a thread, thin and fragile, but strong enough to reel her in, to weave her toward something she couldn't understand.

Without thinking, Selisyn stepped forward.

Her pace quickened as she followed the figure, her heart pounding in her chest, her breath quickening. She wasn't sure why, but she needed to get closer. Needed to understand what it was that kept drawing her in.

The figure turned down an alley, and Selisyn followed. The air seemed colder here, heavier, and the shadows stretched longer as the sun dipped lower in the sky. The alley was quiet, save for the distant hum of the city beyond.

And then, there he was again.

He had stopped at the end of the alley, standing still as though waiting for something, or someone.

Her breath caught in her throat, and she froze, watching him from a distance. He was facing away from her, his broad shoulders silhouetted against the fading light. His presence was magnetic, pulling at her like a gravitational force, but it wasn't just his physicality that captured her attention. It was the way he seemed to radiate something familiar, something that felt like it was woven into the very fabric of her being.

Thalior.

She had never felt so certain of anything in her life. This man, this stranger, was him. There was no doubt.

And yet, there was a strange distance between them. It was as if the world had shifted, separating them in ways she couldn't understand. The memories, the love they had once shared—it all felt so far away.

But still, she was drawn to him.

Her legs moved before she could stop them, and in two quick steps, she was standing just behind him. She didn't know what to say, didn't know how to bridge the gap that had grown between them. All she knew was that she had to reach him.

"Thalior," she said, her voice tentative, though the name felt like it had been carved into her soul.

The figure turned at the sound of her voice, his eyes locking onto hers, wide with an emotion she couldn't name. He stood still for a moment, his expression unreadable, before a flicker of recognition flashed across his face.

He stepped toward her, slowly, almost cautiously. His eyes scanned her, as if searching for something he couldn't quite grasp. His lips parted, but no words came out. Instead, there was only a breath, a breath that seemed to reverberate through the air.

For a long moment, neither of them spoke. The song, that haunting melody, swirled around them, enveloping them both in a soft, wistful embrace. The silence between them was heavy, as though the weight of their shared history pressed down on them.

Then, finally, he spoke, his voice low, almost a whisper.

"I... I know you," he said, the words shaky, uncertain. "I *know* you."

Selisyn's heart clenched, the ache deepening. She didn't know how he knew her. How could he know her when everything between them was gone?

"Do you?" she asked, her voice barely above a whisper. Her eyes searched his, hoping to find something—anything—that would make sense of the feelings swirling inside her.

Thalior took another step forward, his hand outstretched as if to bridge the distance between them. But as he reached for her, a flicker of doubt clouded his gaze.

"I *do*," he repeated, but this time it was more of a question than a certainty.

Selisyn's heart pounded in her chest. She could feel it—the connection. It was there, undeniable. And yet, the more she looked at him, the more the memories eluded her.

"I don't... remember," she whispered, her voice trembling as her hand reached out toward his, though she didn't know why.

He stopped, his fingers hovering just inches from hers. His eyes searched her face, a look of deep sorrow in his gaze, before he whispered, "Then, maybe… maybe we can start again."

The words hung in the air, thick with the weight of all they had lost, and all they still had to find.

The song swirled around them again, louder now, the melody echoing through the alley like the pulse of the earth itself.

And for the first time in what felt like an eternity, they stepped forward—toward each other, unknowingly, pulled together by fate's silent song.

The alleyway seemed to hold its breath as Thalior and Selisyn stood mere inches apart, their hearts beating in sync. The space between them felt electric, charged with an energy neither could explain. The song lingered in the air, its haunting notes wrapping around them, pulling them closer, drawing out the deep, unspoken yearning that lived within them both.

Thalior's hand hovered just above hers, uncertain, as if he was afraid that touching her would shatter something fragile, something they both couldn't yet name. The stillness between them was deafening, the quiet more profound than any noise could ever be. The wind shifted slightly, sending a chill through the air, but neither of them flinched.

"I don't know how to explain this…" Thalior began, his voice raw and unsteady, as if his words were grappling with the weight of forgotten truths. "There's something about you. Something that feels like… I've been waiting for you." His eyes locked with hers, searching, desperate for an answer.

Selisyn's breath hitched. His words stirred something deep within her, an emotion she had not felt in what felt like lifetimes. *Waiting for me.* It was as if those words held the key to everything she had forgotten. Her eyes fluttered shut for a moment, trying to focus on the sensation of his voice, the vibration of his words in her chest.

She opened her eyes again and took a step forward, her fingers trembling, not from fear but from the intensity of the pull she felt toward him. She closed the space between them, finally allowing her hand to meet his, and when their fingers touched, it was as if the world itself exhaled.

For a brief, shining moment, she felt it—*them*—the love they had once shared, the bond that had once been unbreakable. It surged through her like a wave, flooding her with memories she couldn't fully access, but she could feel them. The way he had held her close, the way their laughter had intertwined with the very air around them. The way they had been *one*. It was all there, buried deep beneath the surface of their amnesia, and it hurt—oh, it hurt—because she knew that they were not the same as they once were.

Thalior's grip tightened around her hand, a silent promise hanging in the air. His eyes burned with an intensity that took her breath away. "I don't remember it all either," he said softly, his voice barely above a whisper. "But I feel it. I feel you." He shook his head, a frown tugging at the corners of his mouth. "Why can't I remember everything? Why are we like this?"

"I don't know," Selisyn replied, her voice cracking under the weight of everything they had lost. She could feel it, too—the bond, the echo of their past selves—but it was fragmented, incomplete. It was like trying to grasp a memory that was always just out of reach, like chasing shadows that vanished every time she thought she was close. "But whatever it is, I know it's real. I can feel it, Thalior. I can feel you."

The connection between them was so strong now, the

invisible thread that had once bound them together seemed to stretch across time and space, weaving itself back into place. It wasn't perfect. It wasn't whole. But it was enough to make her believe that they could *find* each other again.

A flicker of uncertainty crossed Thalior's face. He opened his mouth to say something, but the words were lost before they could take shape. He clenched his jaw and shook his head as if to rid himself of the thoughts clouding his mind.

Suddenly, the song grew louder, the notes sharper, more insistent. It reverberated through their bones, a pulse that began to echo in time with their heartbeats. It was almost as if the song was reaching out to them, coaxing them into remembering, into accepting their past and their future.

The song's crescendo surged, and Selisyn felt her body respond to it in a way she couldn't understand. It was as though the very air itself became charged with magic, and the weight of the world around her shifted.

"I know what this is," Thalior said suddenly, his voice urgent, his gaze locked on hers. His hand grasped hers tightly, pulling her a little closer. "This is the song of us, Selisyn. This is the song that has always been there, even when we couldn't hear it." He paused, and his brow furrowed as if the weight of realization was settling on him. "It's the song of our love."

She blinked, taken aback by the clarity of his words. How had he come to this conclusion so quickly? Had he been feeling what she had been feeling, the weight of the connection they shared, even without the memories?

The words felt like a balm to her soul. They *were* the song, weren't they? Their love had always existed, even when it was forgotten, buried beneath the shifting tides of time. It had never truly gone away, even when they had lost each other.

But the real question was—was it enough to rebuild what had been broken? Could they ever go back to the way they had been?

The moment of clarity passed, and once again, the world around them seemed to shift, like a whisper of wind bending the very air. The alleyway began to fade into the distance, the edges of reality blurring as the gravity of their emotions deepened. The city, the streets, the faces—all of it started to dissolve into a murky, indistinct haze.

Selisyn's heart raced. "What's happening?" she asked, her voice shaking as the ground beneath them trembled. "Why is everything—"

Before she could finish her thought, the alleyway was gone, replaced by a vast, swirling void that seemed to stretch endlessly into the unknown. The song filled the space between them, echoing off the nothingness, reverberating deep in their chests. It was more powerful now, the force of it threatening to consume them, to drag them deeper into the abyss.

The void pulsed, as if alive, its energy surrounding them, pulling them toward a singularity they couldn't escape. In the distance, a faint light flickered, but it was so far away, so unreachable. The weight of everything—of their love, of their past, of their broken memories—pressed down on them, and Selisyn's breath hitched.

"Thalior," she whispered, her voice a fragile thread. "What is this? What are we supposed to do?"

He didn't answer immediately. Instead, he took a step back, his eyes wide, his gaze locked on something neither of them could see. The light in the distance flickered again, growing brighter, then dimming in a cyclical pattern. It was like a heartbeat, slow and steady, but filled with an undeniable urgency.

"This… this is where we decide," Thalior said, his voice barely audible, the tension in his words thick with an emotion she couldn't place. His hand slipped from hers, leaving a cold, empty space between them.

"Decide what?" Selisyn's heart beat faster, the song intensifying as the gravity of the situation bore down on them.

"Whether we remember," he said quietly, almost like a prayer, "or whether we forget."

The words hung in the air like an unspoken promise. He was offering her a choice—a choice between a future where they never knew each other again, where their love remained buried beneath layers of lost time, or a future where they rediscovered everything they had been, but at a cost.

A price neither of them was ready to pay.

The light flickered again, and this time, Selisyn knew. It was a choice. A choice that would echo through time itself.

She stood there, frozen, staring at Thalior, feeling the pull of the song, the connection, but knowing that the weight of this decision was far heavier than she had ever imagined.

And in the quiet, with the song swirling between them, the light beckoning them forward, Selisyn realized that the hardest part of all wasn't remembering what they had lost—it was deciding whether to risk everything to find it again.

Eighteen

The Reunion

The winds had calmed, and the storm that had raged for what felt like an eternity finally began to quiet. The once-chaotic skies were now dotted with the soft glow of starlight, the air cool and still as though the world itself had taken a deep, steady breath. Yet, even in this moment of calm, something was different. The earth beneath Selisyn's feet seemed to hum with the pulse of time itself, as if the fabric of existence had been altered, re-woven, and they were now standing at the precipice of something unimaginable.

The ground below her was soft, yielding to her every step, and the world around her shimmered in the afterglow of the destruction—the end of the Singularity, the collapse of everything that had once bound them. The vast expanse of the empty world felt both suffocating and liberating at once. She looked around, her breath shallow, the silence pressing in on her.

The Reunion

And then, she saw him.

Thalior stood a few feet away, his silhouette outlined by the dim, fading light. The storm had left its mark on him, just as it had on her. His hair was tousled, his clothing torn in places, but his presence was undeniable. There was something in the way he stood, the way his eyes were fixed on her with an intensity that sent a shock of recognition straight through her heart.

He remembers.

The thought swept through her like wildfire, a torrent of emotion that nearly knocked her off her feet. Every breath she took seemed to echo the rhythm of a heartbeat that had once been shared between them—before the Singularity, before everything had unraveled. He wasn't just a figure in the distance; he was the other half of her soul, the person who had once been the center of her universe.

Thalior's gaze locked with hers, and a jolt of something—of longing, of relief, of fear—shot through her. He stepped forward, the distance between them closing with each slow, deliberate movement. His eyes were wide, searching, desperate for something that he didn't know how to name. And yet, she felt it too—the pull. The ache of recognition, the yearning to bridge the gap that time and fate had put between them.

"Selisyn…" His voice was hoarse, raw, as if speaking her name was the first thing he had done in an eternity. "It's you. It's really you."

Tears welled in her eyes, unbidden, but she couldn't stop them. The flood of emotion was overwhelming. She took a step forward, then another, and before she knew it, she was standing in front of him, inches apart. His presence was magnetic, a force she couldn't escape, even if she tried.

"Thalior," she whispered, her voice shaking, the name falling from her lips like a prayer. "I don't… I don't know how to…" She trailed off, unsure of how to express the complexity of what she was feeling. The weight of the past, the loss, the absence—it was all there, tangled up in her chest, suffocating her.

He reached out, his hand trembling, and cupped her cheek. The touch was gentle, almost reverent, as though he was afraid she might disappear if he held her too tightly. "I know," he said, his voice thick with emotion. "I feel it too. This… this pull between us. It's like we've always been connected, like we're two halves of the same whole."

Selisyn closed her eyes, leaning into his touch, feeling the warmth of him, the heat of his skin beneath her own. She hadn't realized how much she had missed this. The comfort. The safety. The familiarity. It was like a lifeline thrown into a stormy sea, and she clung to it desperately.

"I remember," he continued, his voice breaking. "I remember everything. The way you laughed, the way we…" He stopped, as if the weight of the words was too much. His hand fell away from her face, but she could feel the lingering touch in the air, like an invisible thread that kept them bound to each other.

"Do you?" she asked, her voice soft but laced with disbelief. "Do you really remember?"

Thalior nodded, his eyes dark with emotion. "I remember you, Selisyn. Every moment. Every second. Even when I couldn't see it, I could feel it. The love, the bond between us. It was always there, even when the world around us was falling apart. And now…" His words faltered, his gaze flickering to the horizon, where the last remnants of the storm were fading into nothingness. "Now we're here, together, and I don't know

The Reunion

what to do with that. I don't know how to fix everything."

The ache in her chest deepened, and she took a step back, wrapping her arms around herself, as though trying to hold herself together. "What do we do now?" she whispered, more to herself than to him.

Thalior's expression softened, but his eyes were filled with uncertainty. "I don't know. But we can't keep running from this, Selisyn. We can't keep pretending that everything that happened doesn't matter. It *matters*. It's everything."

The wind shifted, blowing gently through the ruins of their world. There was no longer a threat of destruction, no more looming darkness. The storm had passed. But in the stillness that followed, a new kind of tension filled the air. Their world had been undone and remade, and now, standing in front of each other, they were left to rebuild what had been lost—not just the world around them, but the love they shared.

A question lingered between them, unspoken but undeniable: *Can we start over?*

Selisyn took a deep breath and raised her eyes to meet his. The intensity of their gaze was like an unspoken vow, a promise that despite the pain, despite the years lost and the memories erased, they would find a way to move forward. She wasn't sure how. She didn't know if they could ever go back to the way things were. But she did know one thing—*this* was real. Their love was real, and it had survived the collapse of everything.

Thalior stepped closer again, this time not with hesitation, but with certainty. His hand found hers, and for a moment, they just stood there, their fingers entwined, letting the silence speak for them. There were no more words to be said—not yet. They didn't need them.

Instead, the world around them began to shift again. The

ground beneath their feet felt solid, the sky above them darkening in the most beautiful way, stars twinkling like a thousand promises. Time, they realized, had started to flow again, and with it came a sense of calm.

Thalior's gaze softened, and he gently brushed a strand of hair from her face. "We can't change what happened," he said quietly, his voice steady but filled with the weight of everything they had endured. "But we can choose what comes next."

Selisyn nodded, her heart swelling with something that bordered on hope. "Yes," she whispered. "We can."

They stood there, in the center of the world they had fought to save, their hands clasped tightly together, the echoes of their love reverberating through the silence. The storm had passed, the battle was over, and now, they faced the unknown together. There was no guarantee of what the future held, no promise that it would be easy.

But for the first time in what felt like forever, Selisyn believed that whatever came next, they would face it—together.

The world around them had settled, but the tension between them lingered like a palpable force in the air. It was the kind of tension that could either pull them together or push them apart. The ground beneath their feet was solid now, but their past—everything they had lost—hung between them, an invisible barrier neither of them had figured out how to break.

Thalior's thumb traced the back of Selisyn's hand, the movement almost imperceptible, but it sent a jolt of warmth through her. He was still there, standing before her, and yet, in some strange way, he felt like a stranger. She had known him, loved him, and lost him. Now, she was supposed to somehow piece together everything that had been erased. The love that had once been so simple, so effortless, was now heavy, weighed down by the enormity of what had happened.

"Do you ever wonder," Thalior asked quietly, his voice steady but tinged with a rawness that made her heart ache, "if we were meant to do this all over again? If our love is cursed, destined to keep coming back only to fall apart?"

Selisyn blinked, her chest tightening at the thought. "I don't know," she said softly, meeting his gaze. "But I do know that it doesn't feel like we should give up. We don't get to choose what the world throws at us, but we can choose what we do with it."

Her words hung between them for a moment, their weight settling into the cracks that had formed in their shared history. She wanted to believe them. She needed to believe that they could overcome the devastation that had followed them like a shadow. But there was always that nagging doubt—was their love truly worth fighting for, or was it doomed to repeat the same cycles?

Thalior's eyes softened, and for a brief moment, it felt as though time had frozen again, just like it had in the Singularity. In that frozen moment, they were the only two souls in the universe, bound together by something neither of them fully understood.

"I don't know either," he admitted, his voice rough, as if the confession had been harder than anything he had ever said. "But I don't want to lose you again. Not like this. Not without fighting."

Selisyn felt her breath catch in her throat. She wanted to say something, anything, but the words escaped her. There was too much—too much grief, too much history. She could feel the remnants of their bond deep within her, pulling at the very core of her being, and yet she was still terrified. She wasn't sure what was scarier: the thought of never seeing him again, or the thought of trying to rebuild something they had already lost.

Thalior took a step closer, closing the distance between them. His hand, still holding hers, tightened ever so slightly, as though he was afraid she would slip away if he didn't hold on.

"I don't want to force you," he said, his voice breaking through the silence that had settled around them. "But if we're given the chance—if we're given the opportunity to rebuild what we had—do you think we can do it?"

The question was like a dagger to her heart. Could they? Could they truly rebuild everything that had been destroyed? Could they erase the pain, the loss, the fear of inevitable separation?

Her heart raced as the weight of his question pressed in on her. She thought back to everything they had been through—the love they shared, the destruction of the Singularity, the sacrifice they had made—and for the first time since it all began, she didn't have an answer.

"I don't know," she whispered. "I don't know if we can, Thalior. But I *do* know that I can't walk away from you. I can't pretend that none of this matters. That we never mattered."

Thalior's face softened, and a slow, wistful smile tugged at his lips. "Then we're not so different after all."

For a moment, they just stood there, the air between them thick with unspoken words. The past—so many moments of joy and pain, of love and loss—had built a wall between them, but now, standing together in the aftermath of the storm, it seemed that wall was crumbling, piece by piece.

The world around them had changed. Time, once shattered,

was now beginning to settle into something new. They were standing on the precipice of something uncertain, something neither of them could predict. But for the first time since the Singularity had collapsed, Selisyn felt something she hadn't in what seemed like forever: hope.

"Do you hear it?" Thalior's voice cut through her thoughts, his expression changing as if something had just caught his attention.

Selisyn frowned, her senses on alert. "Hear what?"

"The song," he whispered, almost as if it were a secret. "It's not gone. It's still here."

A shiver ran down her spine. The song. She had heard it once before, faint and elusive, like a whisper on the wind. And yet, even now, after everything, it seemed to linger in the air around them, calling them, beckoning them forward.

"Is it… is it the same song?" she asked, barely able to keep the tremor from her voice.

Thalior nodded. "It is. But it's different now. Fainter, softer. As if it's fading away with us. But I think it's tied to us, Selisyn. I think it always has been."

Her heart skipped a beat as she processed his words. Could it be that their love, their bond, was still echoing through time, reaching out to them even now? Was it truly the song of their souls, calling them to one another despite everything that had happened?

Without thinking, Selisyn stepped closer to him, her fingers brushing against his, a tentative connection. The world around them seemed to fall away, and all that remained was the sound of their breath, the beat of their hearts, and the song that played just below the surface, a melody only they could hear.

"I don't want to lose it again," she said, her voice trembling.

"You won't," Thalior promised, his grip on her hand tightening. "We won't lose it. Not now, not ever."

For a moment, it felt like time itself had finally caught up with them. The echoes of their love, once trapped in a loop of destruction and rebirth, were now swirling around them like a gentle breeze, filling the empty spaces between them with the possibility of something new.

The storm was over. The Singularity had collapsed. But Selisyn and Thalior? They were still standing, still here, and for the first time in so long, they were no longer afraid.

They were ready to step forward into the unknown together.

Nineteen

The Song Reborn

The world was still, unnervingly still. The storm that had swept through their lives, unraveling time and space, had quieted. There was no wind, no rush of air, no crashing waves of change. Only a thick silence, as though the universe itself was holding its breath, waiting for something to happen. For something to break.

Selisyn stood in the center of the open plain, her body tense, the remnants of time and space swirling in the air around her. The soft glow of the fading stars above painted the world in an ethereal light. It was almost beautiful, in its own way, but there was no peace in the air. It was the calm before an inevitable storm, a storm of their own making.

Thalior stood just a few paces away, his dark eyes fixed on her with an intensity that made her heart ache. They were so close now, yet so far. The distance between them wasn't physical—it was something else, something more intangible.

Their bond, once so strong, so unbreakable, had been shattered and rewritten by time itself. The very thing that had brought them together had torn them apart, over and over again. The memory of their love had been erased, then reformed, and now, standing here, in the aftermath of everything they had endured, the question remained: could they reclaim what they had lost?

Thalior's voice broke the silence, quiet but steady. "Do you feel it?" His eyes never left hers, his gaze unwavering.

Selisyn's heart skipped a beat. She nodded, though the answer wasn't simple. The song—the song that had once bound them together and ripped them apart—was still there, lingering in the air, a faint hum on the edges of her consciousness. She could hear it, feel it. But it was different now. It was no longer a curse. No longer the destructive force it had been. Now, it was something else, something quieter, softer, like a lullaby that only they could hear.

"Yes," she said, her voice barely above a whisper. "But it's... changed."

Thalior stepped closer, his movements slow and deliberate. The air between them seemed to shift, as if the world itself was listening, waiting for the next choice to be made. "It's no longer the song of destruction," he said, his voice carrying a weight that made her chest tighten. "It's the song of rebirth. A chance to start again."

Selisyn's breath caught in her throat. Rebirth. She had never considered it like that, not until now. The song, the song that had broken them, could also be the one to heal them. It could be the key to everything they had lost—if they could learn to listen to it, to understand it. If they could stop fighting against the pull that had always been there, drawing them to one another.

"I don't know if I can," Selisyn said, her voice trembling. She took a step back, her eyes searching his face, but all she saw was uncertainty, fear, hope. "After everything we've been through, can we really rebuild this? Can we rebuild us?"

Thalior's gaze softened, his lips parting slightly as if he were about to speak. But then the air around them seemed to crack, a faint sound breaking the stillness like a distant whisper. The ground beneath their feet shuddered ever so slightly, and Selisyn's heart began to race. The song was growing louder, but there was something else now—a pulse, a beat that echoed with the rhythm of their hearts.

Thalior took another step forward, closing the gap between them. "I don't know what the future holds, Selisyn," he said, his voice low, filled with a mixture of vulnerability and strength. "But I know that I don't want to face it without you. Not anymore."

The words hung in the air, a fragile promise between them. The silence deepened, and for a moment, it was as though time itself paused—suspended in the breathless moment of truth. All that had come before, all the battles, the sacrifices, the endless cycles of loss and rediscovery, all of it led to this.

Selisyn's chest tightened as she looked into Thalior's eyes. She had seen so much in him over the years—strength, courage, love—but now, in the quiet after everything, she saw something new. She saw the reflection of herself in his gaze. A glimpse of the woman she used to be, the one who believed in the possibility of a future. A future with him.

She swallowed hard, feeling the weight of the decision that lay ahead. If they chose to continue, to rebuild what they had, there would be no going back. They could never erase the past.

The scars would remain, deep and permanent. But that didn't mean they couldn't forge something new. Something better.

"I don't know either," Selisyn said finally, her voice steady now, though the uncertainty was still there, buried just beneath the surface. "But I think we have to try."

For a long moment, they stood there, the sound of the song filling the space between them, louder now, pulsing with a rhythm that seemed to be guiding them toward something. Something they couldn't quite see, but could feel with every fiber of their being. The air around them was thick with magic, with power, with the weight of the choice that lay ahead.

And then, without another word, Thalior reached out, his hand trembling as he placed it gently on her cheek. The touch was tentative at first, as if he feared she would pull away. But she didn't. She let him, leaning into his touch, feeling the heat of his skin against hers. Their gazes locked, and for a moment, it felt like nothing else mattered.

The song rose to a crescendo, the melody of their love becoming louder, more insistent. It was as if the world itself was pushing them forward, urging them to embrace what they had been given—a second chance. A chance to rebuild, to reconnect, to heal.

"Are you ready?" Thalior asked softly, his voice barely a whisper, but it echoed in her chest like the beating of her own heart.

Selisyn closed her eyes, her hand finding his, their fingers intertwining. She could feel the warmth of his skin, the strength in his touch. And in that moment, she realized something—something she hadn't fully understood until now.

They were not defined by their past. They were not defined by the destruction, the pain, or the brokenness that had come before. They were defined by their willingness to choose love, over and over again, no matter how many times it had been lost or broken.

"I'm ready," she said, her voice filled with a new sense of certainty, as if the very act of saying the words had changed everything.

Thalior smiled, his gaze softening as he leaned forward, his forehead gently resting against hers. "Then let's rebuild, together."

As they stood there, bathed in the fading light of the stars, the song of their love began to swell, no longer a haunting reminder of what had been lost, but a powerful anthem of what could be. The air shimmered around them, and in the quiet moments that followed, Selisyn felt something shift within her. The past, with all its pain and confusion, no longer held power over her. They had a chance to rebuild—to reclaim their love, their bond, and the future that awaited them.

Together.

The air around them shifted, the space between their hearts narrowing. The faint, ethereal hum of the song swirled like an invisible thread, drawing them closer, pulling them into the very core of what they had once shared. But this time, there was no hesitation, no fear. They were not battling the song; they were surrendering to it.

Selisyn's fingers tightened around Thalior's hand, and the world around them seemed to fade into the background, as if everything else had become irrelevant. All that mattered was this moment—the quiet stillness that existed between the beats of their hearts, the space where the universe held its breath.

The ground beneath them began to pulse, a slow, rhythmic

thrum that matched the beat of the song. It was as if the earth itself was resonating with the power of their choice, the weight of their decision to rebuild what had been shattered.

Thalior lifted his other hand, gently brushing away a strand of Selisyn's hair, his fingers grazing her skin. The touch was tender, almost reverent, as though he feared that even the smallest movement would break the fragile connection between them. But the moment stretched, and she felt the warmth of his hand on her cheek, grounding her, reminding her that they were here, together, and nothing else mattered.

"You're not afraid?" she asked, her voice barely a whisper, though it was as though she had to ask to reassure herself, as much as him.

He shook his head slowly, his eyes soft but filled with determination. "I was afraid once," he admitted. "When we first began this journey, I was afraid of what I might lose, of what might happen if we failed. But now… I realize that love, real love, is not something that can be lost forever. It's never truly gone. It simply waits to be rediscovered."

Selisyn's breath caught in her throat. His words, so simple, yet so profound, struck something deep inside her. She had always feared that they were doomed to repeat the same cycle of pain and loss, that their love would never truly be enough to heal the damage done. But now, in this quiet moment, she understood. They weren't bound by the mistakes of the past. They were free to shape the future, together.

The song swelled, a gentle yet powerful crescendo, vibrating through the very air around them. And then, as though on cue, they both closed their eyes, their hearts aligning with the rhythm of the world.

The earth trembled once more, a soft quake beneath their

The Song Reborn

feet, as if the land itself were awakening from a long slumber. And with that shift, something else stirred within them, something ancient, something powerful—the knowledge that they were not just two individuals finding their way back to one another. They were two forces, two souls bound by fate, standing at the precipice of something much larger than themselves.

A quiet hum filled the space around them, growing louder, deeper. It was the song, but now it was no longer a whisper. It was a full-throated call, a melody that resonated not only in their minds but in their very souls. It was as if the entire universe had conspired to reunite them, to give them this one last chance to rebuild everything they had lost.

Selisyn's eyes fluttered open, and she saw it then—the world around them was changing. The air shimmered, the stars above flickering in time with the pulse of the song. The landscape began to shift, the once barren and broken earth now blossoming with vibrant colors, flowers blooming in rapid succession, the air thick with the scent of new life.

"This is it," Thalior whispered, his voice filled with awe. "This is the power of the song. It's not just us—it's everything. The world, the magic, the love we share. It's all connected."

She nodded, feeling the weight of his words, the truth of them settling deep within her. It was not just their love that had been fractured, but the very fabric of the world itself. Time had unraveled, and with it, so too had the harmony that bound everything together. But now, they were not just mending their bond—they were mending the world.

"Then let's not waste this chance," Selisyn said, her voice steady, but filled with resolve. She turned toward him, her gaze meeting his. "Let's rebuild this world together."

With those words, the final piece of the puzzle clicked into place. The song, the force that had once torn them apart, now began to shift. It was no longer a weapon. It was a bridge—between their hearts, between the past and the future, between all that had been and all that could be.

Thalior stepped forward, his hand finding hers once more, their fingers intertwining. And as they stood there, in the heart of this reborn world, the song grew louder, a powerful, harmonious symphony that filled the air with its resonance. It was a sound unlike anything they had ever heard—a pure, untainted melody that carried with it the promise of everything they had dreamed of and more.

And as the music reached its peak, Selisyn and Thalior were no longer two separate entities. They were one. Their hearts beat in perfect synchrony, the melody of their love weaving together with the rhythm of the world, the song of rebirth filling their very souls.

For the first time, they felt truly free.

But as the song began to fade, replaced by the soft, steady hum of life itself, Selisyn's heart tightened. The world was beginning to stabilize, the magic of the song no longer warping time and space, but the questions still lingered. Could they truly start anew? Or would they forever be haunted by the echoes of the past?

Thalior sensed her hesitation and squeezed her hand gently. "We will face whatever comes," he said softly, his voice filled with certainty. "Together. We don't have to have all the answers. We just have to take the next step."

Her breath caught in her throat, and she nodded, finally understanding. It wasn't about having all the answers. It was about trusting each other. Trusting that their love, their bond, would be enough to carry them through whatever came next.

For the first time in what felt like an eternity, Selisyn smiled. It was a small, fragile smile, but it was enough. Enough to let her believe, just for this moment, that they could rebuild. That the world was not beyond saving. And that maybe, just maybe, their love was more than enough to heal the damage that had been done.

Together, they would face whatever came next, and the song that had once torn them apart would now be the one that carried them forward.

And so, they stood there, hand in hand, as the world around them began to settle, the song fading into the distance, a distant memory of what had been. But in the silence that followed, one truth remained.

The song was reborn. And with it, so too was their love.

Twenty

Eternity's Embrace

The world around them had fallen silent, as though it too was waiting, holding its breath. The echoes of the past reverberated through the air, but they no longer held the weight of destruction. The hollow song, once a haunting force that tore through time and space, now drifted like a whispered lullaby, soft and gentle.

Selisyn and Thalior stood in the heart of this reborn world, the ground beneath them still trembling slightly from the aftershocks of what they had done. The landscape had changed once more, blooming with vibrant colors, the air rich with the scent of life. The world was not perfect, not yet, but it was healing. And they were no longer fighting against time, nor the forces that had sought to tear them apart.

Thalior looked at Selisyn, his eyes tracing the contours of her face, the way the light caught in her hair, the softness in her expression. For a moment, time seemed to stretch out, the years of pain, of separation, fading into nothingness. There was only this moment, the two of them, standing on the precipice of a new beginning.

"I never thought we'd get here," he murmured, his voice thick with emotion, though his words were steady. "I didn't know if it was possible—if we were strong enough to make it through."

Selisyn smiled softly, her eyes filled with the same mixture of relief and awe. She reached out, her hand brushing his, fingers intertwining as though it was the most natural thing in the world. "I didn't either," she admitted, her voice barely above a whisper. "But here we are. Together. And that's all that matters."

The song, now a gentle hum in the distance, seemed to recognize their connection, the way their hearts beat in unison. The air around them shimmered, a delicate spark of magic swirling in the space between them. The world had healed, yes, but so had they. Their love, tested by time and fate, was stronger now than it had ever been. And it was theirs to cherish.

Selisyn could still feel the weight of the past—the memories of their separation, the moments of doubt, the endless cycles of destruction. But they were no longer the defining parts of their story. They had rewritten their future. Together.

And as they stood there, side by side, a new horizon stretched before them—one that they would build, not from the ashes of the old, but from the promise of what could be.

A soft breeze stirred the air, carrying with it the faintest trace of the hollow song, its haunting melody now replaced with a new tune. It was no longer a song of sorrow, but of healing, a tune woven from the threads of hope and renewal. The song had become a part of them, as much a part of their love as the beating of their hearts.

"Do you hear it?" Thalior asked, his voice barely audible over the breeze. "The song… it's different now."

Selisyn closed her eyes, listening to the soft melody that filled the air, weaving its way through the trees, across the fields. It was the same, but not. It was a song of peace, of unity, and of love. It resonated with her, with them, as if it was a part of their very souls. "It's beautiful," she whispered.

The song swirled around them, and with it, a deep, calming warmth settled over her. The tension that had been building in her chest for so long—ever since they had first encountered the song, the echoes of their fractured past, the fear of losing him—began to dissipate. It was no longer a threat. It was a promise.

Thalior stepped closer, his hand still in hers, the world around them shifting as they moved. The ground beneath them was no longer cracked and broken; it was alive with energy, with growth. Flowers bloomed as they walked, their petals opening in the presence of the song's resonance. The air felt thick with magic, as though the very fabric of the realm had been rewoven, rethreaded with purpose.

"This world," Selisyn murmured, her voice carrying the weight of her realization, "it's not just healing because of the song. It's healing because of us. Our choice. Our love."

Thalior stopped, pulling her to a gentle halt. He turned to her, his expression soft but filled with intensity. "It's not just the song," he agreed. "It's us, and everything we've been through. All of it. The pain, the loss, the joy, the love. It's all part of this—of who we are, of what we've become."

A breeze stirred again, and for a moment, Selisyn felt as though the world itself was embracing them, as if the very land beneath their feet had risen to welcome them home. Her heart swelled with a quiet joy, one that transcended words, transcended time.

"We've both changed," she said softly, looking up at him. "And yet, we've never been more ourselves than we are now."

Thalior's lips curled into a smile, but it was tender, almost reverent. "And we will continue to change. Together."

The silence between them was no longer awkward, nor filled with uncertainty. It was a silence of understanding, of acceptance. The world had given them this chance—a chance to rewrite the story, to build a new future, not just for them, but for the realm itself.

The first rays of dawn began to break over the horizon, painting the sky with hues of gold, pink, and lavender. The light, gentle yet radiant, seemed to pour over them, illuminating their faces, their hands still entwined. It was the beginning of something new. A new day. A new world. A new future.

As they stood there, watching the world around them begin to glow with life, they both knew that the path ahead would not always be easy. But it would be theirs to walk. Together.

The hollow song echoed once more, but this time, it was no longer a call of sorrow or fear. It was a lullaby, soft and comforting, a reminder that love, even after all the trials, would always endure.

And as the song's melody faded into the distance, Selisyn and Thalior walked forward, hand in hand, toward a future that they would build together. The realm had been restored, and so had their love.

Selisyn and Thalior walked forward, their hands clasped together as they traversed the now-vibrant world. The colors of the sky deepened, shifting to a rich, glowing orange, as the first true dawn of their new world emerged. The air felt crisp but full of promise, carrying with it the sweet scent of earth and growth. The world around them, which had once been a barren wasteland, was now coming alive. The trees stood tall and proud, their branches swaying gently in the breeze, casting long, shimmering shadows across the land. Flowers, delicate and bright, bloomed at their feet, petals unfurling like a thousand quiet prayers of gratitude.

There was no more rushing, no more frantic need to escape or to fight. Everything felt still, as though time had forgotten how to move too quickly. The balance had been restored, and it felt as though the realm itself was breathing in tandem with them. For the first time in centuries, it felt as though time was their ally, not their enemy.

Selisyn took a deep breath, closing her eyes for a moment, letting the beauty of the world wash over her. The song—the once-agonizing song—now seemed to pulse with contentment. It was a steady, comforting rhythm, like a heartbeat, steady and warm, as though the entire universe had found peace.

"You know," she said softly, her voice barely above a whisper, "I always thought that time would eventually tear us apart. That it would keep us from ever having the chance to truly be together. But now... now I feel like we're part of something bigger. Something timeless."

Thalior's eyes softened as he gazed at her, his face flushed with emotion, his chest heavy with the weight of everything they had endured. "I never thought that I would live to see this day," he admitted, his voice hushed with awe. "I thought it was over for us. That the song, the world, everything we had fought for... it was lost. But now, I see that it was never about defeating time. It was about understanding it."

The two of them stopped at the edge of a river that shimmered like liquid glass, its waters reflecting the new light of dawn. They stood there for a while, taking in the sight of the endless horizon before them, a landscape bathed in soft light, brimming with new possibilities.

"I never thought this world could be whole again," Selisyn murmured. "I thought it was too broken, too far gone. But now… it's beautiful. It's ours."

Thalior turned to her, his face etched with both weariness and peace. He reached for her, cupping her face in his hands, the tenderness of his touch sending a shiver down her spine. "I was wrong," he said quietly. "I thought the world was the only thing that needed to heal. But it was us, all along. We needed to heal, too."

A ripple of emotion coursed through Selisyn, her heart swelling with both love and sadness for all they had lost and all they had gained. The weight of their shared memories, the centuries they had spent apart, pressed on her chest, but there was no longer any bitterness. Only gratitude. Gratitude for their love, for this second chance.

"I love you," she whispered, the words simple but profound, the truth of them resonating deeply within her.

Thalior's eyes glimmered with unshed tears, and for a moment, the world seemed to pause again, the vast, infinite horizon echoing the depth of their connection. "And I love you," he replied, his voice trembling slightly.

They stood together, as the sunlight slowly rose higher, painting the sky in brilliant strokes of gold and lavender. The song, now a low hum in the background, seemed to fade into the distance, no longer the force of turmoil it once was, but a constant companion, a reminder of what they had overcome.

Selisyn took his hand, their fingers curling tightly around one another. Together, they turned away from the river and began walking once more, no longer burdened by the weight of uncertainty, no longer frightened of what the future might bring.

The world around them was still changing, growing, shifting, but now, it was a world that held the promise of a brighter tomorrow. The realm would continue to heal, and so would they. Their love was not a fleeting thing, not something to be erased by time. It had transcended the limitations of time itself. It had become eternal.

And as they walked forward, they knew that the journey ahead was theirs to shape.

The hollow song, now a whisper of joy, followed them as they left behind the shadows of their past. The realm, the world, the song, and their love would endure—forever entwined in the embrace of eternity.

They walked together, side by side, hand in hand, as the new day spread its light across the land. A new beginning had begun, and this time, it would never end.

www.ingramcontent.com/pod-product-compliance
Lightning Source LLC
LaVergne TN
LVHW011937070526
838202LV00054B/4685